University of Michigan Publications

LANGUAGE AND LITERATURE

VOLUME XVII

ELIZABETHAN COMIC CHARACTER CONVENTIONS

ELIZABETHAN COMIC CHARACTER CONVENTIONS

AS REVEALED IN THE COMEDIES OF GEORGE CHAPMAN

BY

PAUL V. KREIDER

OCTAGON BOOKS

A DIVISION OF FARRAR, STRAUS AND GIROUX

New York   1975

Reprinted 1975

by special arrangement with the University of Michigan Press

OCTAGON BOOKS

A DIVISION OF FARRAR, STRAUS & GIROUX, INC.

19 Union Square West

New York, N. Y. 10003

Library of Congress Cataloging in Publication Data

Kreider, Paul Vernon, 1892-
    Elizabethan comic character conventions as revealed in the comedies of George Chapman.

    Reprint of the ed. published by the University of Michigan Press, Ann Arbor, in series: University of Michigan publications, language and literature, v. 17.

    Bibliography: p.
    Includes index.
    1. Chapman, George, 1559?-1634—Technique. 2. English drama—Early modern and Elizabethan, 1500-1600—History and criticism. 3. English drama (Comedy)—History and criticism. 4. Drama—Technique. 5. Characters and characteristics in literature. I. Title. II. Series: Michigan. University. University of Michigan publications: Language and literature; v. 17.

PR2457.C47K73   1975   822'.3   75-11869
ISBN 0-374-94642-6

Manufactured by Braun-Brumfield, Inc.
Ann Arbor, Michigan

Printed in the United States of America

3

To My Mother and My Father

FOREWORD

IT IS probable that the comic writers of the Elizabethan period were students of technique, that the workshops of the theaters were to some extent schools where men studied and applied the known rules of a craft. An examination of the accepted devices throws much light upon the conditions of sixteenth-century dramatic composition, and need not interfere with one's admiration for the frequently beautiful poetry, solid philosophy, and humane emotionalism to be found in the works of the old playwrights. It should be added that many, perhaps all, of the conventions presented in this analysis of comedy are observable in tragedy as well.

The present study is a development of certain sections from a dissertation submitted in partial fulfillment of the requirements for the degree of doctor of philosophy in the University of Michigan. Though conscious of more obligations than can well be expressed, the writer is especially grateful to two scholars, members of the Department of English Language and Literature at that university: Professor Morris P. Tilley, whose friendly and mature counsel has been of inestimable value, and Professor Oscar James Campbell, under whose guidance this investigation was originally planned and through whose encouragement and intelligent criticism it has taken form. Most sincere thanks likewise are due to the editor, Dr. Eugene S. McCartney, for painstaking suggestions on numerous details of mechanical form, and to the Executive Board of the Graduate School for its generosity in providing for the printing of this volume.

P. V. K.

CONTENTS

ix

CHAPTER I

CHAPMAN A TYPICAL ELIZABETHAN DRAMATIST

THE critics are convinced that George Chapman was not a great dramatist. Finding more than enough to disparage in his writings, they have consistently maintained that his plays are neither interesting nor intrinsically important, that whatever value they may possess is historical. Such praise as scholars have been willing to accord to his works has been in many instances only half-hearted; always it has been of limited rather than general application to his plays. In fine, students of Elizabethan drama have created the tradition that Chapman possessed so little virtue as a playwright that it is foolhardy to pretend to have found much value in him.

Active condemnation of Chapman's dramatic ability apparently begins with Dryden's estimate of *Bussy D'Ambois* as "a jelly; nothing but a cold, dull mass, . . . a dwarfish thought, dressed up in gigantic words, repetition in abundance, looseness of expression, and gross hyperboles; the sense of one line expanded prodigiously into ten; and, to sum up all, uncorrect English, and an hideous mingle of false poetry, and true nonsense."[1]

More recent scholars treat Chapman little better. Professor Tucker Brooke, for example, asserts that Chapman's contribution to the development of realistic drama was not the result of artistic sense or of ingenuity; it was sheer chance,

[1] Dedication to *The Spanish Friar*, Scott-Saintsbury edition of *The Works of John Dryden* (1883), VI, 404–405. With this contemptuous opinion Scott is in complete accord (cf. p. 405, note).

"half-blind impulse."[2] Professor Dixon, while he admits that *Bussy D'Ambois* contains some unmistakably good work and feels that Dryden's too stringent criticism is largely the expression of seventeenth-century impatience with Renaissance exuberance, still is no enthusiastic admirer of the earlier dramatist; for his discussion of Chapman opens and closes with the contention that in any period other than the Elizabethan a man possessed of so little dramatic genius as Chapman revealed would not have dreamed of writing plays.[3] Professor Gayley is among those scholars who deny that Chapman displayed any dramatic ability whatever and ascribe to him only historic interest.[4] Denouncing *All Fools* as "primitive" and "puerile," as verbose, superficial, and offensive to good taste, he concludes that the only way Chapman secures any interesting effects is "by transmogrifying character and huddling up poetic justice."[5] He explains that Chapman emphasized the qualities of style and plot then most in vogue, bombast and slapstick humor, wrote only rarely in the fashion of a genuine poet, and by serving stale viands for immediate consumption earned his temporary popularity.[6]

Not all of the criticism, however, has proceeded according to the Dryden formula. Many scholars pay tribute to Chapman's superiority in an art not essentially dramatic, the composition of gnomic and sententious poetry. Professor Brander Matthews recognizes Chapman as one who "had no natural bent toward the theatre," but who was "beyond all question" a poet.[7] Professor Schelling judges that altogether too often

---

[2] *The Tudor Drama*, p. 406.

[3] *The Cambridge History of English Literature*, VI, 33–42.

[4] "A Comparative View of the Fellows and Followers of Shakespeare" (Part One), an essay published in *Representative English Comedies*, II, xi–lix. The discussion of Chapman occurs on pages xlix–liv; the statement referred to is found on page xlix.

[5] *Ibid.*, p. l.   [6] *Ibid.*, p. liii.   [7] *A Study of the Drama*, p. 236.

Chapman's tendency to moralize interfered with the progress of the drama, which must wait until the poetic outburst was over, but that Chapman had the ability to write so eloquently in the gnomic vein that among his contemporaries only Jonson and Greville could compare with him.[8]

Occasionally there appears a critic less concerned with Chapman's confusion of the poetic with the dramatic interest; a critic who consequently pens more laudatory phrases about those powers which this Elizabethan did undeniably display. Professors Neilson and Thorndike concede that Chapman's verse, although often quite inartistic, "at its best . . . is closest of all in its resemblance to Shakespeare's,"[9] while Professor Parrott affirms that Chapman's best prose, as one finds it in *Monsieur D'Olive*, is "second . . . only to Shakespeare's among Elizabethan dramatists,"[10] that his blank verse is more easy and conversational than that of any other poet before Fletcher,[11] and that at least one of his heroines, Margaret in *The Gentleman Usher*, "rises almost . . . to the sphere in which the heroines of Shakespearian comedy move."[12]

Although Chapman at times exhibited unusual poetic talent and although apparently he composed even his comedies with conscientious care,[13] this study of his comedies

---

[8] *Elizabethan Drama*, I, 420. Cf. also Lowell's opinion, expressed in his essay, "Chapman," *The Old English Dramatists*, p. 91, edited by Charles Eliot Norton; scattered comments on pp. 50–51 of A. H. Bullen's article on Chapman in *The Dictionary of National Biography*, Vol. X; and W. Macneile Dixon's criticism in *The Cambridge History of English Literature*, Vol. VI, especially pp. 38–41.

[9] *The Facts about Shakespeare* (Revised Edition), p. 108.

[10] *The Comedies of George Chapman*, p. 781.

[11] *Chapman's "All Fools" and "The Gentleman Usher,"* Belles-Lettres Series, pp. xxxiv–xxxv.

[12] *The Comedies of George Chapman*, pp. 759–760.

[13] An analysis of Chapman's *All Fools* and *Monsieur D'Olive*, for example, demonstrates the fact that the author divided his play with almost

makes no attempt to present Chapman as the poetic or the dramatic equal of Shakespeare. It does not deny, but supports, the critical contention that from the dramatic point of view Chapman exercised so little originality that he cannot be considered much more than a purely conventional Elizabethan. Within the tradition he did show some individuality, and he was awake to experiments in playwriting, but it cannot be proved certainly that he contributed anything to the generally stereotyped technique of his day;[14] he moved, rather, with the progress of his guild.

Within the past two decades or more the altered approach to Elizabethan drama, now generally known as the skeptic attitude and exemplified by such able scholars as Professor Levin L. Schücking in Germany and Professor Elmer Edgar Stoll in the United States, has directed attention more and more to the practical methods of Shakespeare and his contemporaries. It has been represented that the conventions of the Elizabethan theater were definitely set, that they were understood and consistently observed by the dramatic poets, that for the most part they were so obvious and so simple that to the student of Elizabethan drama they should be perfectly transparent, and that the recognition of the prevalence of these mechanical devices will explain many vexing passages in the compositions of even the greatest dramatist of the time. To some extent these standardized practices have been stated and explained; but such expositions, being the result of attention to isolated passages or specific movements within single

---

mathematical exactness between his major and secondary plots, alternated scenes from the two actions as meticulously as did any other Elizabethan playwright, and attempted to fuse the two plots and to make graceful transitions between them.

[14] Chapman's connection with the comedy of humours is discussed in Chapter VIII.

plays, have not been exhaustive. There has been no attempt to determine the extent of the influence of convention in drama and to tabulate the conventions for the sake of greater clarity and certainty of discussion.

Chapman's almost complete lack of originality makes him an excellent playwright for such an investigation. In him, as often is the case with secondary literary figures, the mechanics of dramatic composition are especially patent because he had no very considerable stage genius beneath which to conceal the practical expedients which were the stock in trade of the comic writers of his day. The less unusual he was, the better he serves the present purpose. Chapman employed all the leger-demain of his contemporaries, and few if any methods are observable elsewhere which are not likewise to be discovered in his compositions. Among the relatively numerous works upon Chapman which have been published during the past fifty or sixty years[15] there has been no analysis of the conven-

[15] For example: R. H. Shepherd's edition of *The Comedies and Trag-edies of George Chapman* (1873); William Lyon Phelps's *Chapman*, in the Mermaid Series (1895); Frederick Samuel Boas's edition of *Bussy D'Ambois* and *The Revenge of Bussy D'Ambois* in the Belle-Lettres Series (1905); Thomas Marc Parrott's edition of *All Fools* and *The Gentleman Usher* in the same series (1907); Professor Parrott's numerous articles, such as "The Authorship of *Sir Giles Goosecappe*," *MP*, IV (1906), 25–37, "Notes on the Text of Chapman's Plays. A. *Alphonsus, Emperor of Germany*," and "B. *Caesar and Pompey*," *Anglia*, XXX (1907), 349–379, 501–522, "Notes on the Text of *Bussy D'Ambois*," *ESt*, XXXVIII (1907), 359–395, "Notes on the Text of *The Revenge of Bussy D'Ambois* by George Chap-man," *ESt*, XXXIX (1908), 70–82, his splendid editions of *The Tragedies of George Chapman* (1910) and *The Comedies of George Chapman* (1914); Emil Koeppel's "Quellen-Studien zu den Dramen George Chap-man's, Philip Massinger's, und John Ford's," *Quellen und Forschungen zur Sprach- und Culturgeschichte*, Vol. LXXXII (1897), criticized and augmented by Elizabeth Woodbridge's "An Unnoted Source of Chapman's *All Fools*," *JGP*, I (1897), 338-341, by A. L. Stiefel's "George Chapman und das italienische Drama," *Shakespeare Jahrbuch*, XXXV (1899), 180–213, and by M. Stier's *Chapman's "All Fools" mit besonderer Berücksichti-*

tions observed by this branded conventional and typical dramatist. Because the recent emphasis upon Elizabethan dramatic conventions invites a more comprehensive and more elaborately substantiated exposition of technique than has yet appeared and because Chapman's comedies constitute a fertile territory for the student of Elizabethan dramatic conventions, the present analysis has been undertaken.

In order to keep within bounds it has seemed reasonable to limit the investigation to conventional practices in the presentation of stage characters; that is, in the identification and exposition of characters, including disguised persons and stock figures, with attention to Chapman's reliance upon the psychological notions of his time in his attempt to make his characters clear and convincing. As an outgrowth of this last aspect of the subject, the psychological, a discussion of the comedy of humours has been inevitable.

A further narrowing of the subject has been necessary: the tragic writings of George Chapman have been excluded. Briefly, then, through the analysis of Chapman's comedies[16] this book endeavors to discover and to codify the conventions observed by all Elizabethan comic dramatists in their effort to reveal character. The limits of the subject are set in full consciousness that all mechanical details of this early drama,

---

gung seiner Quellen (1904); Norma Dobie Solve's *Stuart Politics in Chapman's "Tragedy of Chabot"* (1928); W. Bang and R. Brotanek's *Sir Gyles Goosecappe nach der Quarto 1606* (1909); Herbert F. Schwartz's edition of *Alphonsus, Emperor of Germany* (1913); Franck Schoell's edition of *Charlemagne* (1920), his unpublished dissertation on *Chapman as a Comic Writer* (see Parrott's *The Comedies of George Chapman*, p. viii), his article on the authorship of *Charlemagne, Revue germanique* (1912), and his *Études sur l'humanisme continental en Angleterre à la f.a de la Renaissance* (1926); J. M. Robertson's *Shakespeare and Chapman* (1917) and his *The Problems of the Shakespeare Sonnets* (1926); etc., etc.

[16] The comedies considered are those listed in Appendix B, with the

and not merely the identification and exposition of characters, were completely conventionalized and that the playwrights were just as pedestrian, just as subservient to rule of thumb, in tragedy as in comedy. Yet the investigation is made in the hope that the preparation of an analysis of Elizabethan conventions, reasonably exhaustive within the somewhat narrow region arbitrarily defined, may be helpful in the study of English drama of the late sixteenth and the early seventeenth centuries.

---

exception of *Eastward Ho!*, a collaborated piece in which Chapman's part is not certainly identified. *The Ball* is ignored because Chapman had almost nothing to do with it (see p. 165).

CHAPTER II

CONVENTIONAL ELIZABETHAN TECHNIQUE FOR THE IDENTIFICATION AND EXPO-SITION OF CHARACTERS

ELIZABETHAN devices for the identification, exposition, and revelation of stage characters are primitively direct.[1] A new person upon the stage generally is made known promptly by means of remarks of some kind. Frequently when two or more figures make their initial appearance together or when a stranger to the audience joins one or more personages already upon the stage, the dramatist accomplishes the identification simply and naturally by causing his creatures to call each other by name; but in most instances circumstances force the playwright to depend upon methods which are more elaborate and, often, more artificial.

I. DIRECT SELF-IDENTIFICATION

Elizabethan comedy contains many characters who talk much about themselves. Often these naïve egotists, entrusted with the task of making an acquaintance with the audience,

---

[1] A far from complete but suggestive list of references to Elizabethan comic dramatists other than Chapman, illustrating the widespread use of the character conventions discussed in this chapter, will be found in Appendix C. Since the purpose of this study is primarily to reveal and only incidentally (and by inference alone) to differentiate Elizabethan technique, the present chapter considers some practices which, though used extensively in Chapman's period, are not peculiar to it. Various early methods continue, unchanged or in modified form, upon the twentieth-century stage; in some particulars our advancement is revealed by our subtler artifice in concealing technique, not by our utilization of methods in themselves superior.

blandly announce their own names or even impart helpful information concerning their nature and their place in the drama. Such confidences, whether merely self-revelatory or also self-explanatory, occur with equal frequency in monologue and in conversation.

Among the supernumeraries cluttering up the Elizabethan stage there are many figures possessed of no individuality whatever. They are soldiers, gaolers, fools, servants, and so on, presented sometimes singly and sometimes *en masse*, but always labeled conveniently with generic names, as if more distinguishing appellations than "First Citizen" and "First Player" were an unwarranted confusion in the case of characters thus unimportant. Even though specific names may have been assigned to them, such puppets usually prefer to be known in terms of their conventional relationships and predetermined activities. Thus during the first scene of Chapman's *Sir Giles Goosecap* (1601 to 1603)[2] three typical pages introduce themselves to the spectators merely as appendages to their masters, "squires" and "proper eaters,"[3] and the lone page who defends the lively Gazetta in the middle of Chapman's *All Fools* (acted 1599) identifies himself only by stating his function,[4] although all four of these servants are given names in the dramatis personae.

Some Elizabethan personages, however, are as proud of their names as of their type characteristics, especially if the names be indicative of stock traits.[5] In *The Blind Beggar of*

[2] Throughout this study the dates of composition of Chapman's comedies are taken from Professor Parrott's *The Comedies of George Chapman*, the dates of Shakespeare's plays from Chambers' *William Shakespeare*, and the dates of other plays from Chambers' *The Elizabethan Stage*. Appendix B of the present work contains a table of dates suggested by Professor Parrott and others for all of Chapman's comedies.

[3] *Sir Giles Goosecap*, I, i, 45–54.   [4] *All Fools*, III, i, 159–177.

[5] Stock figures are discussed in Chapters IV, V, and VI.

Alexandria (1595–96), when Chapman's Duke Cleanthes demands to be told who is his rival for the hand of Elimine, the ardent suitor both identifies and classifies himself: "I am Signor Bragadino, the martial Spaniardo, the aid of Egypt in her present wars."[6] Childishly frank as this practice is, it was a favorite expedient with even the best dramatists of the period. In one of Shakespeare's latest comedies his prince of vagabonds, apropos of nothing, remarks to the audience: "My father nam'd me Autolycus, who being, as I am, litter'd under Mercury, was likewise a snapper-up of unconsidered trifles";[7] and in Ben Jonson's plays characters as early as Signior Insulo Sogliardo[8] and as late as Sir Politick Would-be[9] speak of themselves with this same lack of reserve.

II. AUTOBIOGRAPHIC SELF-IDENTIFICATION

Sometimes even in the better comedies of the period a character who is entirely undisturbed by the discursiveness of his own remarks narrates the principal events of his life, often including the names and station of his parents. Many of these autobiographic passages are so long and have so little bearing upon the plot that they impress one as narrative material which has escaped from the control of the playwright. In its crudest, least artistic form this method is employed by Chapman when Duke Cleanthes, without making a pretense either of addressing a confidant or of soliloquizing, but frankly speaking to the audience, tells about his parentage, his education, his early activities, and his ambition, and yet manages to associate only a few of these details with the four person-

---

[6] *The Blind Beggar of Alexandria*, ii, 24–25.

[7] *The Winter's Tale* (1610–11), IV, iii, 23–26.

[8] *Every Man out of His Humour* (1599), I, i. Mermaid Series edition of Jonson's plays, I, 129.

[9] *Volpone* (1606), II, i, 24–25.

alities under which he masquerades in *The Blind Beggar of Alexandria*.[10]

Yet by a skillful dramatist this device may be used effectively. Peele's Erestus may recount a moving story of hatred and miserable enchantment;[11] Shakespeare's Aegeon, more concerned about the fortunes of his lost family than about his own fate, may lament the hardships which have driven him finally to despair;[12] and Prospero, at last compelled to speak, may disburden his soul of the dark secrets hidden there for years.[13] These characters possess a depth of experience which Chapman's roguish Cleanthes lacks, and as a result of revealing their not indispensable information concerning past misfortunes they arouse sympathetic interest and gain a touch of nobility permanently wanting in Cleanthes. But in securing these helpful effects Chapman eventually overtook his fellows; for rising above the trumpery of his garrulous shepherd-duke, he bestowed upon Monsieur D'Olive, already characterized as a dolt, a certain amount of dignified, philosophic self-respect when he made that creature declare to Duke Philip that he had deliberately avoided the court all

[10] "I am Cleanthes and blind Irus too,
And more than these, as you shall soon perceive,
Yet but a sheperd's son at Memphis born;
My father was a fortune-teller and from him I learnt his art,
And, knowing to grow great was to grow rich,
Such money as I got by palmistry
I put to use, and by that means became
To take the shape of Leon, by which name
I am well known a wealthy usurer;
And more than this I am two noblemen:
Count Hermes is another of my names,
And Duke Cleanthes whom the Queen so loves."
                                    —i, 110–122.
[11] *The Old Wives Tale* (1591 to 1594), 162–181.
[12] *The Comedy of Errors* (1592–93), I, i, 37–137.
[13] *The Tempest* (1611-12), I, ii, 22–184.

his life because he preferred to dwell in a remote hovel whence, certain at least of a roof above his head, he might view men and matters with absolute detachment and cultivate his mind.[14]

III.   DIRECT SELF-CHARACTERIZATION

Often these egotists are eager to express their inner nature. At the beginning of Chapman's *The Widow's Tears* (1605 or 1606) Tharsalio is alone upon the stage. Without revealing his identity he states the philosophy upon which he is to establish all his undertakings; renouncing Fortune because she is worthy to be venerated only by fools and because she bestows her good and evil blindly, he pledges allegiance to a new deity, Confidence, though Impudence would be a more accurate name for his goddess.[15] He will not passively accept the offerings of circumstance; he will undertake to mold his own destiny. Like Dekker's Fortunatus,[16] Tharsalio carries his opening soliloquy so far that the spectators understand him thoroughly before they know his name. Lorenzo, a completely different character in *May-Day* (1601 or 1602), likewise stamps himself in his first few words. Coming upon the stage while a May Day revel is in progress, this old man so comments upon youthful pleasures that there is no mistaking Chapman's intention of delineating him as a *senex* in

---

[14] *Monsieur D'Olive* (1605?), II, ii, 67–103.

[15]   " . . . thou that lad'st
        Th'unworthy ass with gold, while worth and merit
        Serve thee for nought, weak Fortune, I renounce
        Thy vain dependance, and convert my duty
        And sacrifices of my sweetest thoughts
        To a more noble deity, sole friend to worth,
        And patroness of all good spirits, Confidence."
                                    The Widow's Tears, I, i, 6–12.

[16] *Old Fortunatus* (1599), I, i. Mermaid Series edition of Dekker's works, pp. 293–294.

love.[17] His later absurd philandering is in perfect harmony with the nature which he here assigns to himself. Another elderly father, but with none of Lorenzo's moral irresponsibility, is Dekker's Orlando Friscobaldo. Identified just as he enters, Friscobaldo thereafter talks about himself quite as freely as does Lorenzo.[18]

This method, though far from realistic in that it depicts a person as speaking about himself in soliloquy or in dialogue with a frank self-evaluation of which most people probably are incapable even in thought,[19] still was used freely by the Elizabethan dramatists because it is an easy, swift, sure, and economical way of giving necessary information.

IV. DIRECT SELF-CHARACTERIZATION SUPPLEMENTED
BY A CHORUS

Generally speaking, in Elizabethan comedy all direct characterization, whether uttered by the person depicted or by someone else, is authentic unless it be contrary to facts already established within the play. At times, however, for one comic reason or another the playwright represents an egotist as misjudging himself. But because the author cannot be certain that his auditors will be sensitive to the ironic situation, he must warn them that he does not mean this self-characterization to be accepted as accurate. Under such circumstances the guide is an interpreter, a chorus-like figure who as eavesdropper or as ignored observer placed upon the fringe of the action unequivocally informs his hearers that the speaker is in error concerning his own prowess.

[17] *May-Day*, I, i, 1–25.
[18] *The Honest Whore*, Part II (*c.* 1605), I, ii, 51–99. Friscobaldo does not appear in Part I.
[19] Cf. Schücking, *Character Problems in Shakespeare's Plays*, p. 29, and Stoll, *Shakespeare Studies*, pp. 102, 362–378.

In many cases it would seem as if such an interpreter were unnecessary because the speeches so glossed are obviously sheer braggadocio. Indeed the convention was not followed by so many comic dramatists as were some others, nor was it employed so freely by any single playwright. Yet it was a well-established and persistent practice even among the late writers, especially in deflating the enthusiastic self-characterizations given by such pompous boasters as Beaumont and Fletcher's Prince Pharamond[20] and King Arbaces.[21] For not all noisy self-exaltation is mere vainglory. Many an Elizabethan warrior, scholar, necromancer, or other superman more or less literally makes good his arrogant and extravagant claims, and so the audience was trained to take even bragging seriously. Unless, then, such vaunting speeches as were merely empty noise were properly evaluated by a disinterested choric figure, the spectators might well anticipate that the self-styled hero would justify the character he had given himself. But Elizabethan dramatists are not thus deceptive.

The self-characterization of Lorenzo in *May-Day*, though adequate in itself, is followed immediately by this elaborated method. Just as soon as Lorenzo finishes the soliloquy wherein he asserts that despite his age he retains all the amorous desires and powers of youth, the servant Angelo enters to exercise the choric function. Spying the old Senator, he exclaims aside: "I wonder what made this May morning so cold, and now I see 'tis this January that intrudes into it."[22] Altogether unconscious of the interloper, Lorenzo now begins to reveal the details of his lascivious ambition, boasting of his

---

[20] *Philaster* (not later than 1610), I, i. Mermaid Series edition of the works of Beaumont and Fletcher, I, 107–108.

[21] *A King and No King* (1611), I, i. Mermaid Series, II, 9–10.

[22] *May-Day*, I, i, 26–28.

attractive body and other graces. Then Angelo observes to the audience: "O notable old whinyard."[23] In a few moments, however, the *senex* detects the eavesdropper and attempts to induce him to act as procurer. Lorenzo explains that he is in fact a most lusty reveler, and declares that when the maidens persist in disporting in his presence it is his custom to "give 'em that they come for," and that, too, without unnecessary waste of his precious time; for, says the old Magnifico: "I dally not with 'em." "I know you do not, sir," agrees Angelo; and aside he adds: "His dallying days be done."[24]

Equally ridiculous is the blustering stupid Governor in the last act of *The Widow's Tears*. As chorus Chapman uses Tharsalio, who like many another Elizabethan stage rascal is possessed of a shrewd, practical wisdom far surpassing that bestowed upon any of his fellows in the piece. Hardly has the new Governor spoken his first words when Tharsalio remarks: "Such a creature [a] fool is, when he bestrides the back of authority."[25] Every one of Tharsalio's frequent speeches in this rather long episode refers in some way to the Governor's fatuous ostentation.[26]

V.   PRELIMINARY DIRECT CHARACTERIZATION

Neither Chapman nor any other typical Elizabethan dramatist, however, entrusts the entire responsibility for characterization to persons who talk about themselves. Much more frequently a sixteenth-century playwright gives detailed information through speeches assigned to others. The bulk of this material, and that which is most enlightening, occurs early in the play. Such exposition is direct and succinct, and the device is so simple and efficacious that often the spectators gain a considerable amount of knowledge of a character

[23] *Ibid.*, I, i, 45–51.

[24] *Ibid.*, I, i, 130–137.

[25] *The Widow's Tears*, V, iii, 238–239.

[26] *Ibid.*, V, iii, 219–345.

long before they see him for the first time. For mannikins possessed of only one characteristic, such as Middleton's Lucre[27] and most of Chapman's puppet-like figures, a single fairly well constructed explanation is sufficient. But as these stage creatures become more pretentious, less limited to the strict confines of a type, and as the playwright attempts to make the purpose of his dialogue less obviously mechanical and to impart verisimilitude to it, the expositions are more conscientiously managed and also more numerous. Indeed the master dramatist may finally reach the point where he devotes a series of carefully designed passages to the delineation of a character as developed as Shakespeare's Olivia,[28] though this latter development is an expansion and nicety of technique to which Chapman does not attain.

In the most direct manner Chapman devotes a large part of the first scene of *Sir Giles Goosecap* to the characterization of the eccentrics who are never more than grotesque marionettes and who do not come upon the stage before the second scene.[29] Captain Foulweather is called "a dull moist-brained ass.... As fearful as a hare, and 'a will lie like a lapwing."[30]

[27] *A Trick to Catch the Old One* (1604 to 1606), I, i. Mermaid Series edition of Middleton's works, I, 5–9.

[28] *Twelfth Night* (1599–1600). Olivia first appears in I, v, but she is discussed in every preceding scene and in the early part of the fifth. In I, i, 23–41, Shakespeare elaborately characterizes her as sentimentally emotional, overserious, and indifferent to Orsino's love. This information is repeated in I, ii, 34–46, and to it is added a statement of the popular good opinion of her. Her seriousness, quietness, and regard for decency are emphasized in I, iii, 1–17; and in I, iii, 111–117, is revealed her modest good judgment. The characteristics divulged in I, i, are implied as the basis for I, iv; and even in I, v, 1–4, 17–18, 33–34, immediately before Olivia enters, Shakespeare further enriches this already extensive characterization by introducing the element of sternness.

[29] *Sir Giles Goosecap*, I, i, 55–127. For the significance of scenes such as this, which exploit oddities without advancing or even touching plot, see Chapter VIII.   [30] *Ibid.*, I, i, 68–80.

Foulweather's page declares that Sir Cuthbert Rudesby is blunt and defiant in manner, uncouth and ferocious in appearance.[31] More skillfully Chapman prepares for the parasite Medice, in *The Gentleman Usher* (1602), through whose villainy the rivalry of Duke Alphonso and his son, Prince Vincentio, for the love of Margaret develops almost tragically. About fifty lines before Medice's first entry, Vincentio and the courtier Strozza describe Medice as a "fustian lord," a base and poverty-stricken pretender, an illiterate hanger-on barren of honor, who has somehow wormed his way into the Duke's favor.[32] Chapman prepares his hearers not only to understand the character but also to guess something of the personal appearance of this man; for Strozza says that Medice's face is "a map of baseness," and Vincentio asserts that the parasite dresses like a footman. Surely there can be no difficulty in identifying this creature and no uncertainty about his character when he appears.

VI. DIRECT CHARACTERIZATION IMMEDIATELY PRECEDING FIRST APPEARANCE

Frequently this anticipatory characterization, instead of being given in earlier scenes or episodes, is postponed until the moment immediately preceding the first appearance of the person discussed. After an expository speech, simple or elaborate, which terminates with such a remark as "Here he is now," the new figure comes upon the stage. This method, a favorite with Chapman and his contemporaries (among

[31] " . . . blunt Sir Cut. Rudesby, is indeed blunt at a sharp wit, and sharp at a blunt wit; a good bustling gallant, talks well at rovers; he is two parts soldie; as slovenly as a Switzer, and somewhat like one in face too; for he wears a bush beard will dead a cannon-shot better than a wool-pack; he will come into the presence like your Frenchman in foul boots, and dares eat garlic as a prep[a]rative to his courtship."— I, i, 120–127.

[32] *The Gentleman Usher*, I, i, 107–127.

them Day[33] and Jonson[34]), is one of the few character conventions that have been discussed by students of Elizabethan drama.[35] Economical in that it both identifies and characterizes a personage, it is so compact and so pellucid that intelligence of the lowest order could not misunderstand it.

Blanuel, in Chapman's *An Humourous Day's Mirth* (1597), never develops, never becomes dramatically important; conceived as an automaton, he has no opportunity to escape from his limitations. But the dramatist carefully explains precisely how this puppet works. The courtier Lemot describes him as a "complete ape" whose social equipment consists only of two tricks, repeating what others have said and assuming melancholy, and then his anatomist draws his remarks to a focus by announcing: "See where he comes."[36] When the introduction is concluded, Blanuel stands before the audience.

In Chapman's *All Fools* Cornelio comes upon the boards with the same kind of introduction. His wife Gazetta reveals the ugly secrets of their domestic unhappiness. She tells a companion that Cornelio is obsessed by an unreasoning jealousy, a practical determination to believe himself betrayed; and yet, she declares, this farmer husband is so eager to make his way with the gallants of the city that he wastes his wealth in gaming with the very men he suspects and even entertains

---

[33] See the exposition of Aspero in *Humour out of Breath* (1607–8), I, ii. Mermaid Series, *Nero and Other Plays*, p. 279

[34] See the elucidation of the character of Sir Amorous LaFoole, *Epicœne* (1609), I, iii, 22–49. In Professor Gayley's text the characterization ends the scene; but the following scene opens with LaFoole entering to join the group of men who have just spoken of him, and of course upon the Elizabethan stage there would thus be no pause between the exposition and the appearance of the character.

[35] See, for example, Schücking, *op. cit.*, pp. 53–54, and Wilhelm Creizenach, *The English Drama in the Age of Shakespeare*, pp. 282, 284.

[36] *An Humourous Day's Mirth*, ii, 23–51.

them in his home. As she finishes this analysis, Cornelio comes out of the house and she says: "See, see, we shall be troubled with him now."[37]

VII. DIRECT CHARACTERIZATION DURING OR SUBSEQUENT TO FIRST APPEARANCE

Very often the Elizabethan comic dramatists, introducing a slight modification, characterize a figure not before his initial appearance but during or immediately after it. While he is still in full view or else the moment he has departed, and consequently while the first impression is strong in the minds of the spectators, other persons upon the stage impart the desired information in such a way as to remove any uncertainty or misconception about him. The method has the additional advantage of appearing to be entirely natural, since the exposition develops from a stage situation. Character revelation of this kind was always popular with the playwrights: Lyly employed it early in describing Silena;[38] much later Dekker and Webster used it to depict the Chamberlain, that "honest knave . . . called Innocence";[39] and after years had passed Thomas Heywood was building upon the same technique in his presentation of Bess Bridges.[40]

In *May-Day* Chapman wishes to distinguish old Gasparo as miserly, and the young hero, Aurelio, as capable, intelligent, and likable. Lorenzo, when he spies Gasparo, turns and says to his comrade: "Away, here comes a snudge that must be my son-in-law."[41] Later in the same scene Aurelio is so overcome by the sight of his mistress that he falls to the

[37] *All Fools*, I, ii, 20–42.
[38] *Mother Bombie* (1587 to 1590), II, iii, 8–75.
[39] *Northward Ho!* (1605), I, i. Dyce's *Webster*, p. 249.
[40] *The Fair Maid of the West* (date uncertain; not later than 1617), I, iii. Mermaid Series edition of Heywood's works, p. 85.
[41] *May-Day*, I, i, 163–164.

ground in an agony of love. Directly Lodovico and Giacomo enter and, seeing Aurelio prostrate, suppose that he is intoxicated. Then Lodovico expresses his deep regret that the vice of drunkenness should be found in a man who is endowed with such gentlemanly virtues as intelligence, education, handsomeness of person, and valor.[42]

Chapman pursues the same course with even more vigor in *Monsieur D'Olive*. When Mugeron sees D'Olive, he brands him "fool,"[43] as Lorenzo calls Gasparo a "snudge." Then after D'Olive has swaggered to his exit, Roderique enlarges upon Mugeron's relatively mild characterization.[44] He supplies much more information concerning his subject than D'Olive's antics have yet suggested; in fact he gives details which are not illustrated by any of D'Olive's subsequent action in the play. Chapman develops the conception of this eccentric figure more by supplementary statements than he does by exposition of the man as the audience has seen him, or is to see him at any time.

VIII.   LATER DIRECT CHARACTERIZATION

Direct characterization through the speech of other figures does not always terminate when the person leaves the

---

[42] "What a loathsome creature man is, being drunk! Is it not pity to see a man of good hope, a toward scholar, writes a theme well, scans a verse well, and likely in time to make a proper man, a good leg, specially in a boot, valiant, well-spoken, and, in a word, what not?" —I, i, 197–202.

[43] *Monsieur D'Olive*, I, i, 258–259.

[44] "Farewell, the true map of a gull! . . . 'Tis the perfect model of an impudent upstart, the compound of a poet and a lawyer; . . . Oh, 'tis a most accomplished ass, the mo[n]grel of a gull and a villain, the very essence of his soul is pure villainy; the substance of his brain, foolery; one that believes nothing from the stars upward. A pagan in belief, an epicure beyond belief; prodigious in lust, prodigal in wasteful expense, in necessary most penurious; his wit is to admire and imitate, his grace is to censure and detract." —I, i, 392–414.

stage after his first appearance. Expository passages are often found scattered throughout the play, even last-minute characterizations occurring, though with less frequency in comedy than in tragedy.[45] There is a bit of closing explanation or summary of character in *The Gentleman Usher*, a comedy so nearly tragic that it may reasonably borrow details from tragic technique. After the villainy of Medice has become apparent even to the beguiled Duke, the court openly turns upon the parasite, and clown and pages, crying "My lord Stinkard" and "Fox," beat him from the presence.[46]

When the characterization is not thus postponed to the very end of the comedy, that is, when the audience is still learning to know a creature who will continue to reappear from time to time, the dramatist generally gives more detail. Early in *May-Day* the gay young Lodovico comments freely upon Gasparo, whom Lorenzo has already called a "snudge." First Lodovico emphasizes Gasparo's advanced age; then he draws attention to his dirtiness and various other offensive physical qualities; next he discloses Gasparo's impoverished, rustic origin and his rapid acquisition of wealth through usury; and finally he states that the old scoundrel's ambition is to marry into a family far superior to his own.[47] Similarly, although Tharsalio has portrayed his own nature in the opening soliloquy of *The Widow's Tears*, yet a few scenes later his brother Lysander adds perspective to the picture by explaining that it is because of bad associates and evil practices that Tharsalio has lost all respect for womanhood, humanity, and God.[48]

In these instances, as in Porter's complete analysis of Moll

[45] For example, *Othello* (1604–5), V, ii, 338–361; *Julius Caesar* (1599–1600), V, v, 68–75; *Hamlet* (1600–1), V, ii, 406–411; *Antony and Cleopatra* (1606–7), V, i, 13–48, and V, ii, 79–92.
[46] *The Gentleman Usher*, V, iv, 271–282.   [47] *May-Day*, II, i, 64–78.
[48] *The Widow's Tears*, II, i, 46–54.

Barnes[49] and the unknown author's description of Frank Jerningham,[50] and indeed generally in Elizabethan comedy, the playwright is concerned with static personages. But sometimes, as with Chapman's Lemot in *An Humourous Day's Mirth*, conditions are different. After behaving for some time as a purely conventional intriguer, Lemot suddenly displays a new and dangerous quality: he becomes "the very imp of desolation," a man in whose presence no woman is safe.[51] This expanded delineation is a preparation for Lemot's ensuing action, the seduction of Florilla, canting Puritan wife of the old and impotent Labervele.

IX. NARRATIVE FOR PURPOSES OF CHARACTERIZATION

Sometimes long narrative passages are used to reveal the nature either of the person telling the story or of someone else in the play. In comedy these tales are generally humorous enough to have been introduced for their comic value alone, but at the same time they often accomplish a distinct and necessary character exposition.

In Chapman's *All Fools* Gostanzo displays all the comic weaknesses of the conventional irritable father. Among his foibles is his contempt for his son Valerio, a contempt based upon the old gentleman's mistaken belief that the youth is backward in the company of ladies. In order to inspire Valerio to greater manliness, Gostanzo, under the impression that he is giving an account of irresistible social cleverness, actually describes the *gaucherie* of his own early manners; and his present silly delight in his callow juvenility casts a farcical light over him, exposing at once his persistent lack of good

---

[49] *The Two Angry Women of Abington* (not later than 1598), v, 10–39.
[50] *The Merry Devill of Edmonton* (*c*. 1603), I, iii, 106–111.
[51] *An Humourous Day's Mirth*, iv, 136–140.

sense.[52] In the same scene, soon after this first narrative self-revelation, there occurs a similar long anecdotal passage spoken by Valerio and intended by the dramatist to set at nought the father's representation of Valerio as weak and diffident. The boy roars with laughter as he describes how, beset by bailiffs and hemmed in by lawyers, he turned upon the pack, sword in hand, and drove them pellmell down the stairs.[53] The contrast between Valerio as Gostanzo unhappily believes him to be and the same young man as his close comrades know him is further pointed out by the playwright; for as Valerio and his companions enter, one of them is saying to him:

> Well, wag, well; wilt thou still deceive thy father,
> And being so simple a poor soul before him,
> Turn swaggerer in all companies besides?[54]

The result of these two narratives is that Gostanzo, who has set out to describe his son as a ninny, actually has revealed himself as an incurable rustic and that Valerio has shown himself to be an unrestrained roysterer.

Among Chapman's half-wits is the blunderer Poggio in *The Gentleman Usher*, who differs from most figures who present themselves through anecdotes in that he tells stories not of what he has actually experienced but of what he has dreamed. He explains how be became angered in his dream and, having begun to beat his enemy, stubbornly refused to waken until he had sufficiently thumped him. It is indeed part of Poggio's fatuousness that he is incapable of making any distinction between reality and a dream.[55]

Although Chapman used these anecdotes only to depict ridiculous characters, some of his contemporaries occasionally employed the same technique to present the more sober fig-

---

[52] *All Fools*, II, i, 147–178.   [54] *Ibid.*, II, i, 296–298.
[53] *Ibid.*, II, i, 296–335.   [55] *The Gentleman Usher*, I, i, 1–48.

ures of comedy. The yarn spun by Jenkin the Clown in *The Pinner of Wakefield*[56] is ludicrous self-characterization, but Scudmore's amorous reverie in Field's *A Woman is a Weathercock*[57] is intended to reveal a comparatively serious spirit. Shakespeare, with his usual versatility, employed the tale for both kinds of effect; for his account of Katherina's smiting of her music-teacher[58] and his report of Petruchio's conduct at his own wedding[59] are comic characterizations, while the story of Jaques and the wounded deer[60] serves to present a man who is grotesque, eccentric, and amusing and yet must be accepted as a person primarily serious.

X. CHARACTER VERIFIES GENUINE CHANGE OF HIS
OWN ATTITUDE

In Elizabethan drama it often happens that during the course of a play a personage undergoes, or craftily pretends to undergo, alteration. Either a genuine or a feigned shift of attitude imposes a new responsibility upon the playwright, who, having carefully built up one conception of the figure, must now guide the audience successfully while the established characterization is altered or unavoidably jeopardized. Here again the author relies upon transparent devices to inform the spectators of the real state of the character's mind.

When the personage is undergoing a genuine alteration, he so informs the audience through the soliloquy or the aside. In Chapman's *The Blind Beggar of Alexandria* Queen Aegiale is in love with Duke Cleanthes, but the King has

[56] Greene's (?) *George a Greene, The Pinner of Wakefield* (not later than 1593), lines 374–435.
[57] *A Woman is a Weathercock* (1609?), I, i. Mermaid Series, *Nero and Other Plays*, p. 345.
[58] *The Taming of the Shrew* (1593–94), II, i, 143–160.
[59] *Ibid.*, III, ii, 151–184.
[60] *As You Like It* (1599–1600), II, i, 25–66.

discovered the intrigue and has driven Cleanthes into exile. Aegiale has longed for her lover; now he returns in disguise, and without making his identity known to the Queen he advises her to kill her husband if she would recover the Duke. After he has departed Aegiale delivers a soliloquy to explain, in psychological terms, her reaction to the sinister suggestion, and ends by setting in motion the scheme which is to result in the death of the King.[61] Her pining has changed to active manipulation of circumstances, and her soliloquy has established the sincerity of the transformation.

The Countess Eudora, heroine in the secondary action of Chapman's *The Widow's Tears*, is deaf to the entreaties of all suitors. Tharsalio, who is baffled and rejected like the rest, at last employs the bawd Arsace to tempt Eudora for him; and under the guise of friendliness the depraved agent advises the Countess to shun Tharsalio because of his reputation as a vigorous and insatiable male. This appeal to the widowed lady's dormant passion is successful; she promptly decides to marry Tharsalio, and she communicates her decision to the audience in a brief speech after Arsace has left.[62]

This kind of exposition has the weakness and the strength always attaching to the aside and the soliloquy; the method itself is blatantly artificial, but the information so given is never open to question. For want of a better way of securing equally satisfactory results the dramatists resorted to this practice throughout the Elizabethan period: Greene, writing just as the major dramatic movement of the time was getting under way, used an aside to verify the change in Prince Edward's attitude toward Lacie and Margret;[63] and Dekker, in the early years of the first Stuart monarch, assigned to Or-

---

[61] *The Blind Beggar of Alexandria*, vi, 1–88.
[62] *The Widow's Tears*, II, ii, 56–136.
[63] *Frier Bacon and Frier Bungay* (*c.* 1589), viii, 112–121.

lando Friscobaldo a soliloquy for the express purpose of assuring the auditors that the old gentleman had experienced a complete reversal of feeling toward his daughter Bella-front.[64]

When changes of attitude on the part of comic figures of the times are only a pretense, the playwright uses the same care that his audience be not misled, and he guides his spectators by the same devices as when the character alterations are genuine. The person who pretends to be changing says plainly, in soliloquy or aside, that in reality his feelings are unmodified.

In *An Humourous Day's Mirth* old Labervele, although affecting for politic reasons to wish that his gay young wife Florilla would wear jewels and mingle freely with other people, is in fact just as jealous and suspicious as he always has been. His apparently docile wife accepts his proposal as an honest expression of his desires, and promises to oblige him by doing as he has suggested. Immediately Labervele mutters in a perturbed aside that he has not expected her to accept his recommendation.[65] This single expository speech exposes the husband's duplicity and so interprets the entire episode.

Margaret, heroine of *The Gentleman Usher*, receives a letter from her lover, Prince Vincentio. The messenger, Margaret's complacent usher Bassiolo, urges his lady to compose a favorable reply. Finally, apparently persuaded much against her will and judgment, she dispatches Bassiolo with an answer. As soon as the gentleman usher is conveniently

---

[64] *The Honest Whore*, Part II, I, ii, 208–225.
[65] *An Humourous Day's Mirth*, iv, 45–86.

out of hearing, Margaret laughs at him, declaring in a soliloquy that her love for the Prince is deep, genuine, and of long standing, that her unexpected reluctance is mere trickery to fool Bassiolo.[66]

For the woodcocks upon the stage there are many springes; but lest the woodcocks among the auditors entangle themselves therein, the dramatists who devised these traps, both before and after Chapman, frequently warned of their location. When in *Endimion* Tellus agrees to accept the love of Corsites after he has accomplished what she knows to be an impossible task, Lyly gives her a soliloquy in which she states that she has taken this means of ridding herself of her troublesome suitor.[67] And Shakespeare's Cressida, during those salad days when she is still so green in judgment that the appearance of modesty seems worth preserving, befuddles the accommodating Pandarus much as Chapman's Margaret deceives Bassiolo.[68]

A complicated and most interesting modification of this kind of scene is developed in Chapman's *All Fools*. In the struggle of wits between Valerio and Rinaldo and their fathers, Gostanzo and Antonio, the young intriguers have been forced to abandon their pretense that Gazetta is the wife of Fortunio, Rinaldo's brother and Antonio's son. They therefore tell Gostanzo the truth, that she is Valerio's bride, but impart the information in such a way that he believes the story is only a ruse to deceive Antonio. Gostanzo immediately reveals the supposed fraud to Antonio. When finally the youths and their fathers come together, the sons carry out their gulling as they have planned, while the fathers, secure in their mistaken interpretation of the situation, apparently

[66] *The Gentleman Usher*, III, ii, 524–529.
[67] *Endimion* (1588), IV, i, 72–79.
[68] *Troilus and Cressida* (1601–2), I, ii, 308–321.

change the attitudes which they have maintained up to that time. Actually they utter asides which not only indicate that their feelings are as they have been, but, further, show how completely the fathers are outwitted by the young rogues. Each faction is fooling the other, but in the end, as conventionally happens in intrigue comedy, the younger men get what they want at the expense of the older ones.[69]

XII. INTERPRETATION SUPPLIED BY CHORUS AT TIME OF CHANGE OF ATTITUDE

In more elaborate fashion Elizabethan comic dramatists at times interpret a change of attitude through the mouth of a character acting as chorus. The employment of the choric personage in the exposition of a static figure has already been discussed. When the method is expanded so as to explain a shifting character, the changed—or, more generally, changing—person plays his part in a straightforward manner, while an observer upon the stage gives the audience a true understanding of the action. This directive comment is especially helpful in a scene which represents someone like an intriguer, either benevolent or malign, attempting to effect a change in the mind of someone else. Since ordinarily the intriguer keeps more or less in the background, it often happens that he himself acts as chorus.

Dowsecer, son of Labervele in *An Humourous Day's Mirth*, is a melancholy young man whom his father and others successfully attempt to rouse from his depressed humour. Part of their activity consists in placing a portrait of the engaging young lady, Martia, where Dowsecer must see it. As he is inspired by the picture to escape from his dejection and to adopt a normal point of view, Labervele and his

---

[69] *All Fools*, IV, i, 75–220. The careful preparation for this episode is found in III, i, 1–129, 428–446, and IV, i, 1–75.

confederates stand at the back of the stage watching and making comments on the alteration in Dowsecer's mind. These interpretations are not designated as asides, but Dowsecer is the focus of interest and they are a part of a separate conversation which serves to assure the audience that a genuine, beneficial change is occurring before them.[70]

In *Monsieur D'Olive* Marcellina has taken a vow to live in seclusion because her husband, Vaumont, has accused her of infidelity. Vaumont and his friend Vandome devise a plan which they believe will induce her to reënter the world. While Vandome works upon the feelings of the injured wife and her companion Eurione, Vaumont, who is supposed to be far away in grave personal danger, actually is hiding upon the stage and uttering asides.[71] By following his comments the audience learns what progress Vandome is making in his effort to move Marcellina. In other words Chapman uses this eavesdropper to indicate the various points in the modification of Marcellina's attitude; and such information is authentic. This scene is suggestive, in mechanics rather than in art, of Shakespeare's most gratifying use of the convention, the passage in *Measure for Measure* which represents Isabella before Angelo pleading for her brother's life while Lucio, stationed beside the maiden, explains the effect her speeches are making upon the Deputy's mind and urges her to greater effort.[72]

In *Monsieur D'Olive* there is a man as sentimental as Marcellina, the widower St. Anne, who has long refused to bury his wife's body. Finally aroused by the discovery that Eurione resembles his dead wife, he regains his interest in the living and determines to marry again. This information

[70] *An Humourous Day's Mirth*, vii, 134–219.
[71] *Monsieur D'Olive*, V, i, 10–219.
[72] *Measure for Measure* (1604–5), II, ii, 25–161.

Chapman imparts in a curious way. First of all Vandome asserts in soliloquy that such a change has taken place in the spirit of St. Anne; then as if to confirm the rumor St. Anne enters and, unaware of Vandome's presence, declares, in what he supposes is a soliloquy, that he has fallen in love with the lady Eurione and intends to marry her. Vandome remarks aside that this confession indicates a genuine change on St. Anne's part. After some further soliloquizing which amounts to a feeble moral struggle, St. Anne states his final resolution and then Vandome joins him.[73] Thus the scene is developed by a composite method; the character verifies his own change of attitude and in addition the choric figure certifies the accuracy of the revelation both before and during the time it is made. In a sense the two men are vouching for each other's statements. A somewhat similar composite eavesdropping occurs in Middleton's *Michaelmas Term* when Quomodo and his "spirits" are filching Easy. The sharpers observe and accurately report the various shifts in the victim's mind, designating the somewhat complicated fluctuations which eventuate in his succumbing to their guile. At the same time Thomasine, Quomodo's wife, who later helps Easy to baffle the swindler, is standing unobserved and offering comments which corroborate those made by the swindlers.[74]

Further variations of this method are found in Chapman's comedies, especially where a change of attitude is not genuine. While Franceschina, wife of the braggart captain Quintiliano in *May-Day*, is in tears because her husband talks of going to the wars, Angelo in an aside explains that behind her hands the lady is not weeping but laughing.[75] Since this episode constitutes the whole of Franceschina's first appear-

---

[73] *Monsieur D'Olive*, IV, i, 1–49.
[74] *Michaelmas Term* (1606?), II, iii, 103–389.
[75] *May-Day*, I, i, 279–303.

ance, Angelo's comment is largely characterization; and yet it shows that Franceschina's grief is only a pretense and that her actual feeling is a continuation of that first ascribed to her when in a brief preliminary passage it was intimated that she was the mistress of Angelo.[76] In *An Humourous Day's Mirth* Labervele, acting as choric character, so misinterprets a feigned change of attitude that he reveals himself as a person completely beguiled. He has been justifiably suspicious of the friendship between his Puritan wife Florilla and the court rake Lemot. And now Florilla, with the intention of giving her husband a feeling of security so that she may safely pursue her wanton delights, persuades Labervele to overhear a conversation between herself and her seducer. When Lemot appears and works upon Florilla's passions, the old husband stands aside as expositor of the effect of these wicked suggestions upon his own wife. But through a series of asides Labervele so completely misinterprets what he sees and hears that his comments are most patently ridiculous.[77]

[76] *Ibid.*, I, i, 90–96.
[77] *An Humourous Day's Mirth*, vi, 1–135. For a brief consideration of Epithetic Direct Characterization, not discussed in this chapter, see the latter part of Appendix C.

CHAPTER III

MANAGEMENT OF DISGUISED CHARACTERS

NO SINGLE plot device is used in Elizabethan comedy more generally and more continuously than is disguise. Until shortly after the death of the Queen, the dramatists labored just as conscientiously to reveal the identity of disguised personages as they did to identify unmasked figures at the time of their initial appearance and to characterize them throughout the play. Either ignorant of the fact that disguise is seldom more than mildly convincing upon the stage or else disregarding it, they punctiliously observed the very obvious conventions which they had developed for the presentation of masquerade.[1]

Disguise, however necessitated, is always adopted as a means of deceiving someone; and customarily those who adopt it are, like their brother tricksters the intriguers, at least temporarily successful.[2] The fact that masking is sup-

---

[1] A list of references to a few cases of disguise presented by dramatists other than Chapman will be found at the end of Appendix C. M. L. Arnold, *The Soliloquies of Shakespeare*, pp. 56–58, discusses the soliloquy as one of Shakespeare's methods of exposing hidden identity. Wilhelm Creizenach, *The English Drama in the Age of Shakespeare*, pp. 220–223, summarizes various disguise motifs and lists examples. The writer has an exhaustive analysis, "'The Mechanics of Disguise in Shakespeare's Plays," in the *Shakespeare Association Bulletin*, IX (1934), 167–180. See also V. O. Freeburg's *Disguise Plots in Elizabethan Drama*.

[2] This generalization applies to tragedy as well as to comedy. To illustrate only from Shakespeare, Iago's plotting and Kent's disguise are not detected until too late; Othello has murdered Desdemona by the time he discovers Iago's villainy; and Kent keeps his secret so well that, when

posed to conceal the identity of the one who attempts it places certain limitations upon the means available for imparting information concerning disguised persons. Unless other characters are fellow conspirators, they cannot know, and so cannot reveal, the identity of the masquerader. Indeed part of the comic effect of a disguise is often secured by depicting some person as ridiculously blind to a perfectly transparent subterfuge.[3]

The remaining possibilities of naming masked figures, however, are adequate. The early methods may be grouped under four heads. In the first place it is always possible for the masquerader to name himself and thus to effect a speedy and absolute identification. Again the person may adopt his disguise, may actually put it on, while standing upon the stage in full view of the audience. Often, too, a character discusses in detail the disguise which he is about to assume. This third method, elaborate preparation, is probably the most constant part of the entire disguise technique of the meticulous dramatist and may be presented either through the

---

finally he would reveal himself to Lear, the old king is too far gone to understand the situation. Edgar's disguise and Edmund's scheming progress as planned; but Tybalt's recognition of the masked Romeo will be recalled as a rare instance of the defeat of an attempt at concealment. In comedy the disguises of Viola, Rosalind, Portia, Imogen, Vincentio, and others are not penetrated; the substitution of Mariana for Isabella, as of Helena for Diana, meets no obstacle; and the more active intriguing of Don John, Iachimo, and Maria and her confederates prospers sufficiently.

[3] For example, when Falstaff is dressed as the old woman of Brainford, Evans notices, apparently without suspicion, Falstaff's "great peard" (*The Merry Wives of Windsor* [1600-1], IV, ii, 202-205); and Chapman's Quintiliano, seeing his own wife dressed as a page and in the company of her lover, knows immediately that she is a woman, but does not for a moment suspect she is Franceschina, and so chuckles at the joke which he sees this light woman playing upon her doting and complacent husband (*May-Day*, IV, iii, 114-133; IV, iv, 1-23).

medium of soliloquy or through conversation between the masker and his comrade in disguise or his confederate in the plan. Finally the masquerader may have a confidant, frequently a page or a jester, who helps to devise the plot and who, undisguised, accompanies the trickster and so, either through appropriate speech or merely through his presence, helps the auditors to recognize his companion. Generally the situation is so elaborately developed that a combination of these methods, rather than any single one, is used.

Disguise bulks large in three of Chapman's comedies: *The Blind Beggar of Alexandria* (1595–96), *May-Day* (1601 or 1602), and *The Widow's Tears* (1605 or 1606). The dramatist's devices are different in the three plays and, analyzed chronologically, they demonstrate transition from the most rudimentary expedients, through elaborate and self-conscious technique, into complacent sophistication.[4]

Among the four favorite methods of divulging concealed identity the most naïve are self-identification and the adoption of the mask while in full view of the audience. These practices constitute the machinery of mumming in Chapman's earliest comedy. When the central figure of *The Blind Beggar of Alexandria* makes his initial appearance, he is Irus, destitute and blind but pious. So propitious are the events of the first scene, however, that his intended victims have scarcely withdrawn when he discloses his resources and his villainy. While disguising himself as Count Hermes, he discusses his costume and the accompanying personality which he assumes, and states that he is also Duke Cleanthes.[5] In the

---

[4] As the discussion in this chapter will show, there is no consistent desertion of simple forms of revelation of identity, and no consistent adoption of more subtle practices, in Elizabethan comedy.

[5] *The Blind Beggar of Alexandria*, i, 324–343:

    Irus: Now to my wardrobe for my velvet gown;
    Now doth the sport begin.

second scene Irus wears the garments which he donned during the closing lines of Scene i.

In the third scene Irus presents another impersonation; there he is Leon the usurer. As soon as he comes upon the stage in this new nature, he says, "Now am I Leon, the rich usurer";[6] and twice during the next twenty-five lines he states that he is the man sometimes known also as Cleanthes.[7] His actual appearance as the Duke is postponed, however, until the final scene of the play; although in the preceding scene Chapman makes careful preparation for the coming of that personage when Leon, hearing the public clamor for the return of the exiled warrior, twice declares his intention of reassuming the "form and shape" of Cleanthes.[8] As Scene x begins the Duke leads in his prisoners of war and introduces himself to the audience by means of a self-identification only slightly less direct than those he used when he appeared as Hermes and Leon.[9]

> Come, gird this pistol closely to my side,
> By which I make men fear my humour still,
> And have slain two or three, as 'twere my mood,
> When I have done it most advisedly,
> To rid them, as they were my heavy foes.
> Now am I known to be the mad-brain Count,
> Whose humours twice five summers I have held,
> And said at first I came from stately Rome,
> Calling myself Count Hermes, and assuming
> The humour of a wild and frantic man,
> . . . . . . and this gown I wear
> In rain, or snow, or in the hottest summer,
> And never go nor ride without a gown;
> Which humour does not fit my frenzy well,
> But hides my person's form from being known,
> When I Cleanthes am to be descried.

[6] *Ibid.*, iii, 28.   [7] *Ibid.*, iii, 28–52.   [8] *Ibid.*, ix, 139–155.
[9] The Duke informs his prisoners that they have been overcome by Cleanthes and must yield their crowns to him; the four kings swear allegi-

Throughout the comedy Chapman keeps the changing personality of this character clear by simple means. For example, from time to time he emphasizes the fact that several persons are one man under different names;[10] he plays up the blustering humour of the "mad-brain Count";[11] and even in one scene in which the central personage functions successively as Leon, Hermes, and Irus, the playwright so announces each of the several appearances that there is no confusion.[12]

A less elaborate disguise in the same play is that of the secondary figure, Irus's brother and serving-man Pego, who is known also as the Burgomaster. His part is a minor one and Chapman's preparation for the masquerade consists of three simple details: Irus thrice refers to Pego as his brother, at the same time announcing that he has made Pego Burgomaster, and Pego addresses Irus as "good master brother";[13] when Pego enters in disguise he again calls Irus "master brother," and Irus, now dressed as Count Hermes, names Pego "Master Burgomaster";[14] and both Irus and Pego emphasize the fact that they are disguised.[15]

Mumming runs entirely through Chapman's later play, *May-Day*, the collapse of a masquerade leading swiftly to the formulation of a second. In addition to these major disguises, *May-Day* contains two instances among the supernumerary personages and one transient incident founded upon mistaken identity. In this comedy Chapman no longer relies

---

ance to their conqueror, sometimes, in their vows, using the second personal pronoun, and sometimes using the name "Cleanthes."—*The Blind Beggar of Alexandria*, x, 1–30.

[10] For example, *ibid.*, i, 143–144, 349; v, 75–76.

[11] For example, *ibid.*, vi, 9–20; vii, 22–44; ix, 7–44. In the first two of these passages the gown in which Irus disguised himself as Hermes in Scene i is mentioned; in the first there is also mention of the pistol put on at the same time; in the third passage the name "Count Hermes" is used as well as the epithets "wicked" and "bloody"; in the first passage he is the "rude Count" and in the second the "mad-brain Count."

[12] *Ibid.*, iv, 41–182. [14] *Ibid.*, i, 344, 346.

[13] *Ibid.*, i, 129–147. [15] *Ibid.*, i, 349, 356.

upon the callow simplicity of his earlier technique.[16] Characters no longer name themselves; the dramatist's practices have become less mechanically artificial.

The most elaborate attempt at concealed identity in *May-Day* develops in a wholly farcical manner as the result of old Lorenzo's passion for Franceschina, the young wife of Captain Quintiliano. Angelo, Franceschina's lover, compelled against his will to become an intermediary for Lorenzo, determines to whet the Senator's senile appetite for the sake of the merriment the situation will afford. He induces the lady to accept the infatuation as an opportunity for mirth, and so secures her consent to admit her aged suitor to her home. Angelo guarantees to avoid any scandal by bringing Lorenzo so completely disguised that no neighbor will have any suspicion.[17]

As Franceschina leaves her lover, Lorenzo appears. Angelo immediately broaches the subject of a disguise. Lorenzo demurs; this antic is beneath the dignity of a Magnifico, but in the end he agrees. The plotters discuss the masquerade in detail: Lorenzo shall appear as Snail, the chimney-sweep; he shall wear old and sooty garments; he shall sing a bawdy song as he trudges the streets; and he shall besmirch his face beyond all possibility of recognition. Then shall he enter the home of his Franceschina, doff his soiled clothing, wash his hands and face, feast, and revel.[18] Every conceivable detail

[16] Although the plot incidents of *May-Day* are adapted from Alessandro Piccolomini's *Alessandro*, the advancement in Chapman's technique cannot be credited wholly to the influence of the Italian dramatist. (Cf. Parrott, *The Comedies of George Chapman*, pp. 732–737.)

[17] Angelo's promise to Franceschina constitutes the first mention of disguise in connection with the Lorenzo action. It occurs in *May-Day*, II, i, 387–394. The entire conversation between Angelo and Franceschina occupies lines 358–402.

[18] *May-Day*, II, i, 402–520. In lines 475–489, there occurs an interesting comment upon stage disguises in Chapman's time. Lorenzo has suggested that he disguise himself as a friar. "Out upon't," retorts Angelo,

of the man's assumed appearance is emphasized in this long preparatory dialogue.

In the next scene the nature of Lorenzo's disguise is stated three times,[19] once by the intriguer Angelo himself, who then departs to prepare the Senator for his adventure. As soon as the third person has announced the masquerade, Angelo brings Lorenzo onto the stage with the disguise half effected. The Magnifico is still daubing his face with soot; but finally he is content to take the implements of his pretended trade. He draws attention to his garb and his newly mastered street cry, and starts away singing as he has heard Snail do.[20] Immediately the gallants of the city accost him. Feigning ignorance of his identity, they address him as Snail and make remarks uncomplimentary to both the chimney-sweep and the Senator.[21]

In a moment Angelo and Lorenzo are shown before

"that disguise is worn threadbare upon every stage, and so much villainy committed under that habit that 'tis grown as suspicious as the vilest. If you will hearken to any, take such a transformance as you may be sure will keep you from discovery; for though it be the stale refuge of miserable poets by change of a hat or a cloak to alter the whole state of a comedy, so as the father must not know his own child, forsooth, nor the wife her husband, yet you must not think they do [in] earnest carry it away so; for say you were stuffed into a motley coat, crowded in the case of a base viol, or buttoned up in a cloak-bag even to your chin, yet if I see your face, I am able to say, 'This is Signor Lorenzo,' and therefore unless your disguise be such that your face may bear as great a part in it as the rest, the rest is nothing."

[19] *Ibid.*, III, i, 1–89. The repetition of this information occurs in a scene essentially comic. Angelo reports the plot to Lorenzo's nephew, Lodovico, who promises not to reveal the secret; as soon as Angelo departs, however, Lodovico shares the news with young Honorio; and Honorio, in spite of his pledge of silence, instantly relays the story to Gasparo. All three of these men plan to torment the disguised Lorenzo. The scene may have been constructed for its comic value alone; but it is characteristic of Chapman's repetition for the sake of emphasis, and, intentionally or otherwise, makes confusion impossible.

[20] *Ibid.*, III, i, 90–141.   [21] *Ibid.*, III, i, 142–227.

Quintiliano's home. Angelo addresses the masker as "your worship" and reminds him that he has deceived even his own nephew. In his reply the *senex* again draws attention to the fact that he is attired as a chimney-sweep only so that he may seduce Franceschina. And later the lady and her lover refer to the Magnifico as an "old flesh-monger," a "horseman" who must be punished for his inappropriate ambition.[22] In this scene the presence of the fellow-conspirator Angelo assists in the unmistakable identification of the masquerader.

When next Lorenzo appears he is dragged in by the infuriated Captain Quintiliano, who has discovered him in Franceschina's coal room. The husband accepts the intruder as the chimney-sweep, but threatens violence because of Snail's evil reputation. Lorenzo pleads innocence, Franceschina cannot be found, and Quintiliano releases the culprit. During his few moments of jeopardy, however, the Senator twice mutters to himself: "A plague of all disguises!" Here, in addition to utilizing the expedient of having Lorenzo seized in the place where Franceschina had previously vowed she would imprison him,[23] Chapman further elucidates the action by making the prisoner twice refer to himself as one disguised.[24] And when the aged adventurer appears in disguise for the last time, running home in terror of Quintiliano's wrath, he is still declaring: "A plague of all disguises," while Angelo, again present, assures him that only a disguise has saved his reputation.[25]

Thus it appears that in this instance Chapman, while still unnecessarily and perhaps monotonously cautious, uses methods which are more advanced than the simple self-identification employed, with other methods, in *The Blind Beggar of*

[22] *Ibid.*, III, ii, 1–45.   [23] *Ibid.*, III, ii, 37–38, 43–44.
[24] *Ibid.*, IV, i, 49–99. "A plague of all disguises!" 73, 95.
[25] *Ibid.*, IV, ii, 25–66.

Alexandria. In *May-Day* he gives repeated preliminary information concerning the nature of the disguise which is to be adopted; he has the mummer assume part of his disguise while upon the stage; he provides the masker with a confederate who not only, by his presence, identifies the Magnifico, but also addresses Lorenzo as one of much higher rank than a chimney-sweep; and he makes both Angelo and Lorenzo refer to the disguise constantly in conversation, and the Senator himself in asides.

Angelo's interest in the Lorenzo-Franceschina fiasco is due in part to the fact that the old Senator's absence from his home enables Angelo's master, Aurelio, to visit his sweetheart, Lorenzo's daughter Aemilia. This assignation is abruptly terminated, however, by the disguised father's unexpected return. As Angelo follows the fleeing Magnifico through the streets, he foresees trouble for the young lovers; and from this danger arises the second mumming in *May-Day*, the masquerade of Franceschina as a man.

Once Lorenzo has reached the door of his own home, Angelo in vain attempts to dissuade him from entering. The old rascal quickly reappears in the street, announcing that he has discovered a man in Aemilia's chamber. Determined to call officers to apprehend his daughter's paramour, he reënters his house to remove his disguise. Immediately Angelo sets to work upon a new scheme. After hustling his master home to change clothes, Angelo announces to the audience that he will take Aurelio's garments to Franceschina, induce her to don them, and then send her to Aemilia's room, where she will be found by Lorenzo.[26] When Aurelio and Angelo return to the stage, the former is just completing his change of clothes and is urging Angelo to hasten to Franceschina.[27]

[26] *May-Day*, IV, ii, 40–109.
[27] *Ibid.*, IV, ii, 163–201. The fifty-four lines intervening between this

Toward the end of the following scene Angelo and Franceschina, the lady now in disguise, make their appearance. Angelo serves here again to identify the masked character, partly because the audience knows his plans perfectly and partly because he addresses Franceschina as "coz" and "wench," kisses her, and declares she takes the part of a page excellently. To further the matter, Chapman makes this couple enter while Quintiliano and Innocentio are present. Franceschina in a sense identifies herself when she says to Angelo: "God's pity, my husband!" And Quintiliano points out to Innocentio the evidence that this apparent page is some "wench in man's attire."[28]

With the next scene Angelo is sending Franceschina up the ladder to Aemilia's window. He repeatedly calls her "coz" and reminds her that she is "short-heeled." As soon as she has vanished through the window and Angelo has slipped around the corner of the house, the Captain and Innocentio come up, lamenting the fact that they have lost sight of the gallant and his masquerading "stale punk," as Innocentio calls her. Instantly two serving-men are upon the stage, talking about Franceschina's male attire and her visit to the home of Lorenzo.[29] In a later scene there is some reference to the masquerade of Franceschina and also to that of Lorenzo; but it has significance as part of the intrigue movement rather than as a device for explaining disguise.[30]

Within this farcical maze of mummery is found also an undeveloped romantic tale of two young lovers who, exiled from their homeland, have concealed their identity and have even misrepresented their sex. These persons are Theagine and Lucretio, who have assumed the names Lionello and

and the preceding reference are given over to an entirely separate disguise motif, to be discussed later.

[28] *Ibid.*, IV, iii, 114–133. [29] *Ibid.*, IV, iv, 1–35. [30] *Ibid.*, V, i, *passim.*

Lucretia. Their part in the action is negligible, and practically nothing is revealed about them until the closing scene of the play. The maiden Theagine, disguised as page to Leonoro, makes several brief appearances, but has few and insignificant speeches only. A mere attendant upon Leonoro with no part of her own, she never compels any interest, even though Chapman finally makes an uninspired attempt to arouse some curiosity about her by permitting her to hint vaguely that she is not a page but a woman in disguise.[31] When Lionello-Theagine next appears, in the final scene of the play, the dramatist develops a conventional recognition scene in which both Theagine and Lucretio tell the stories of their lives and so complete the identification.[32] At the time of his first appearance, however, the disguised Lucretio has intimated that he is a man.[33] And during his second turn upon the stage he has imparted additional information; he has stated his name and admitted that he is living in exile, but has refused to say more.[34] His self-revelation, as well as that of Theagine, is crassly completed in the recognition scene already referred to.[35]

The dramatist, then, displays no such mature hand in the

---

[31] *Leonoro* [who has requested Lionello to disguise as a woman]: Come, Lionel, let me see how naturally thou canst play the woman. *Exit*
    Lionello: Better than you think for.
                        —*May-Day*, IV, ii, 243–245.

[32] *Ibid.*, V, i, 243–276

[33] *Ibid.*, II, i, 34–40.   [34] *Ibid.*, IV, ii, 117–141.

[35] For a statement of the original of this disguised-lover action, and for Professor Parrott's comment on Chapman's superiority to Piccolomini in the presentation of it, see Parrott, *op. cit.*, pp. 733–735. Although Chapman shows more skill than his predecessor, he displays little or no inventive cleverness as he retells the story. Such revelatory information as the playwright gives before the last scene is imparted through strained devices, especially in the case of Lucretio. And the recognition scene, even in the classical comedy, where it is essential to the principal action, is unnatural and unconvincing enough.

Lucretio-Theagine plot as he does in the Lorenzo disguise or even in the Franceschina mummery. From the beginning the characters in this inconsequential action are in masquerade.[36] There is no preliminary discussion of a costume still to be adopted, no changing of garments upon the stage, no helpful outpouring of information to a confederate, unless indeed the quaking Lodovico[37] be metamorphosed into a confidant. The guidance given the audience consists of hints at concealed sex and then blunt self-identification. But one element of the most sophisticated Elizabethan technique does appear in this apparently careless development of the theme: the playwright, whether through lack of interest in the miniature plot, or because of a feeling that the matter of identity has little bearing upon the tenuous romantic story, or possibly in harmony with some more or less conscious progress toward a changing method, keeps the identity of the lovers secret as well as he can and so introduces into the disguise motif the detail of mystification and mild surprise.

The management of disguise in Chapman's last comedy, *The Widow's Tears*, is quite different from that found in the two earlier plays. Lysander is so confident of the chastity of his wife Cynthia that he accepts Tharsalio's challenge to put her to the test. Having set out upon a journey, he sends his servant back home to report his death and then returns in disguise to await developments. Cynthia retires to Lysander's tomb with the avowed intention of fasting there until she

---

[36] There is an even less important episode in this play, based upon concealed identity rather than disguise. Lodovico, muffled in his cloak, is mistaken by the bawd Temperance for another gentleman and conducted into the chamber of Lucretia, where his experiences are entirely farcical. —*Ibid.*, III, iii, 118–179; IV, ii, 110–161.

[37] Lucretio, infuriated by Lodovico's insolence, attacks him with a sword, and in his angry speech reveals his own name and state. —*Ibid.*, IV, ii, 110–141.

dies; but Lysander, in the guise of a soldier, enters the tomb and seduces his own wife.

Although the customary expository passages are wanting in this comedy, Chapman keeps the identity of the masquerader reasonably clear. Lysander adopts his disguise not early in the play, as do many other characters, but at the beginning of the Fourth Act, by which time his voice and features are thoroughly known and the audience has become perfectly familiar with his trusting and chivalrous attitude toward women, especially toward his wife. At the beginning of the scene Lysander enters, according to the stage direction, *"like a Soldier disguised at all parts; a half-pike, gorget, etc."*[38] After descanting upon the wonder of women in general and the celestial qualities of Cynthia in particular, and after expressing sorrow and disgust that men should doubt the integrity of womanhood, Lysander enters the tomb.[39] In spite of his entreaties and his mockery, he cannot induce his wife to eat or even to pay any heed to him. At the end of the scene, when he is again alone, Lysander delivers an even more enthusiastic panegyric upon Cynthia's matchless purity.[40] The dramatist thus introduces the husband fully disguised and does not take the precaution to insert into either of the soliloquies any such reference to Lysander's relation to Cynthia as would constitute a direct self-identification. He does, however, attribute to his hero a characteristic attitude and an interest in the widow to distinguish him from anyone else in the play.

The ensuing scene represents Lysander within the tomb, still disguised, after Cynthia has so far broken her vow as to eat and drink what he left for her upon the occasion of his first visit; but there is no word which could in any way expose

---

[38] *The Widow's Tears*, stage direction preceding IV, ii, 1.
[39] *Ibid.*, IV, ii, 1–14.   [40] *Ibid.*, IV, ii, 180–187.

the masquerader to an audience not already aware of his identity.[41] By the time he departs he has won the widow from
every pretense at constancy. The disillusioned husband's disgust is expressed in language appropriately extravagant; but
beyond the bitterness of his denunciation there is only his
reference to Cynthia as "this mirror of nuptial chastity, this
votress of widow-constancy," and to "her husband's supposed
body," and his contemptuous assertion that this paragon of
virtue has succumbed to the solicitation of an "eightpenny
soldier," to indicate that the seducer is actually the husband.[42]

The last important scene in this action begins as Cynthia
is about to open her husband's coffin with a crowbar. Lysander's life is in danger because while he was carousing with his
mistress-wife someone stole the body of a criminal from the
cross which Lysander has been ordered to guard. Cynthia is
eager to save her lover by substituting the body of her husband for that of the crucified malefactor. During this relatively brief episode Lysander is given four violent asides;[43]
and when he emerges from the tomb he throws his armor
away, exclaiming, "Off with this antic, the shirt that Hercules
wore for his wife was not more baneful."[44]

Although this removal of the disguise in the presence of
the audience would dispel any lingering uncertainty concerning the soldier, Chapman carries the story still further.
Lysander's brother Tharsalio has witnessed some of the love-
making between Cynthia and the guard, but has not recognized Lysander.[45] Now that the infuriated husband has
foregone his soldiering, Tharsalio comes upon him in the
graveyard. It is only after some unsatisfactory conversation
with his brother that Tharsalio realizes what has occurred.

[41] *Ibid.*, IV, iii, 41–86.   [42] *Ibid.*, V, i, 114–123.
[43] *Ibid.*, V, ii, 13, 18, 58, 60.
[44] *Ibid.*, V, ii, 61–62. The soliloquy occupies lines 61–76.
[45] *Ibid.*, V, i, 22–80.

Thereupon Tharsalio, in soliloquy, marshals the evidence which proves that the guard and Lysander are one person, and then restates the details of the disguise story, thus employing the conventional Elizabethan narrative résumé as a final identification.[46]

Chapman's method in *The Widow's Tears* demonstrates what was referred to above as the technique of complacent sophistication. Ignoring the more naïve practices—direct self-identification, the assumption of the disguise upon the stage, preparatory discussion of the masquerade, and even the use of a confidant—the dramatist recognizes stage mummery as a well-nigh constant convention, apparently feels secure in assuming the playgoer's familiarity with it, and leaves something to the ingenuity of the auditor. He unravels his story in a less artificially mechanical manner, yet with sufficient clarity for the average intelligence, even though disguise actually were as baffling for the audience as the playwright pretends it is for the characters upon the stage. He reverts to primitive safeguards only with the termination of the action.

All the methods used by Chapman in presenting his disguised characters are employed either simply or in modified form by his contemporaries. The most obvious device, direct self-identification, is illustrated, for example, in the masquerade of the Second Luce in *The Wise-Woman of Hogsdon*[47] and in the various subterfuges of Jonson's Justice Overdo[48] and Lanthorn Leatherhead.[49] For none of these disguises is there the slightest preparation, but the audience is given the necessary guidance by the characters themselves who, as soon

[46] *The Widow's Tears*, V, ii, 81–129.
[47] Thomas Heywood, *The Wise-Woman of Hogsdon* (*c.* 1604?), I, i. Mermaid Series edition of Heywood's works, pp. 263–264.
[48] *Bartholomew Fair* (1614), II, i; V, ii. Mermaid Series edition of Jonson's works, I, 37, 126.
[49] *Ibid.*, V, i. Mermaid Series edition, I, 125.

as they appear upon the stage, or, in the case of Luce, as soon as opportunity offers, reveal their own identity.

The second, less frequently utilized practice, that of assuming the disguise within view of the audience, is Shakespeare's method in connection with the foolery of Feste[50] and the knavery of Autolycus.[51] It is used, too, by Dekker in explaining the action of Orlando Friscobaldo.[52] It is impossible to permit a personage to change his garments and alter his features upon the stage without at the same time allowing him to make some remarks concerning his plans and concerning the nature of his disguise. And so preparatory discussion is a complementary element in this method.

Such a preparatory discussion, carefully manipulated, becomes an indispensable part of the third set of mechanics. And since such expository material generally is delivered in conversation rather than in soliloquy, this process is closely linked to the fourth possible expedient, the use of an undisguised confidant who serves to establish the identity of the masker. Greene's Dorothea goes into some detail in planning the male attire which she intends to assume,[53] as do also Rosalind,[54] Portia,[55] Imogen,[56] and various other Shakespearean heroines. Among those whose change of garments does not involve concealment of sex, Celia in the appearance of a shepherdess[57] and Raymond Mounchensey in that of a friar[58] make the same preliminary use of the confidant.

[50] *Twelfth Night* (1599–1600), IV, ii, 1–11.
[51] *The Winter's Tale* (1610–11), IV, iv, 635–697.
[52] *The Honest Whore*, Part II (c. 1605), I, ii, 233–257.
[53] *James the Fourth* (c. 1591), III, iii, 99–135.
[54] *As You Like It* (1599–1600), I, iii, 113–135.
[55] *The Merchant of Venice* (1596–97). III, iv, 57–84.
[56] *Cymbeline* (1609–10), III, iv, 168–196.
[57] *As You Like It*, I, iii, 113–135.
[58] Anonymous, *The Merry Devill of Edmonton* (c. 1603), II, ii, 76–77; II, iii, 69–78.

It will be recalled that some of these mummers, on their first appearance in masquerade, are accompanied by undisguised attendants, often the persons with whom they planned the escapade. Nano, who has helped Dorothea with her garb, reappears with her when she presents herself as a page.[59] Rosalind and Celia escape in the attire of country folk, taking Touchstone with them;[60] and while the jester has not helped to organize the expedition toward Arden, he has been mentioned as a companion for the journey. Moreover these two women, disguised as they have previously explained, manage to identify each other, as do the two young legal gentlemen, Portia and Nerissa. The first dialogue of the masquerading characters in *As You Like It*[61] and in *James the Fourth*[62] is of such nature as to expose the masker.

When the mummer is deprived of the assistance of the confidant, he sometimes is compelled to explain himself to the audience, and generally he does so promptly and unequivocally. Thus because the accomplice in *Cymbeline* and in *The Merry Devill of Edmonton* aids only in planning the disguise and not in identifying the concealed personage, Imogen soliloquizes upon the hardship of leading a man's life much as Rosalind confesses womanhood in her conversation with Celia and Touchstone,[63] and it is left for Raymond Mounchensey himself to deny that he is actually a holy man.[64] On the other hand the dramatist frequently substitutes for the accommodating confidant a character who, ignorant of the fact that there is any masquerade, unwittingly utters remarks which reveal the disguised person to the auditors. Orsino, for example, comments at length upon the feminine attractiveness

---

[59] *James the Fourth*, IV, iv, 1–19.   [60] *As You Like It*, II, iv, 1–10.
[61] *Ibid.*   [62] *James the Fourth*, IV, iv, 1–19.
[63] *Cymbeline*, III, vi, 1–27.
[64] *The Merry Devill of Edmonton*, III, ii, 12–25, 71–88.

of Cesario, although the Duke has no suspicion that his page is a woman,[65] and Margret senses a courtliness that distinguishes the high-born Lacie from the clowns among whom he appears.[66]

Often, especially in plays of later date, both the preparatory exposition and the process of revelation are noticeably slight. In Shakespeare's *The Winter's Tale* Polixenes twice declares that he and Camillo, attired in some unexplained disguise, must watch the ill-advised courtship of Florizel.[67] When the two gentlemen reappear, moreover, there is no direct identification of them, though their conversation is such as to catch the attention of the wary. The brief episode concludes with the king removing his disguise.[68] In similar fashion Heywood's Bess asserts that she will play a trick on Roughman; she does not say what it is to be, nor does she imply that it will involve a masquerade.[69] When she is ready to dupe her enemy, she appears disguised as a page and sets out in the company of the apprentice Clem, who has had no part in devising the scheme but who now helps to carry on a conversation which discloses the fact that this young swaggerer is a woman.[70] After Clem departs, Bess speaks a brief soliloquy on her "immodesty" and on her disguise.[71] During her quarrel with Roughman, however, she reveals neither her name nor her sex.[72] Much later in the play she says openly that it was she who, as a page, administered a beating to the ruffian.[73] In Middleton's *Michaelmas Term* the varied dis-

---

[65] *Twelfth Night*, I, iv, 30–34. Cf. also 41–42.

[66] *Frier Bacon and Frier Bungay* (*c.* 1589), iii, 59–74. For this disguise and the three preceding ones there is somewhat detailed preparation.

[67] *The Winter's Tale*, IV, ii, 52–54, 61.   [68] *Ibid.*, IV, iv, 55–428.

[69] Thomas Heywood, *The Fair Maid of the West* (acted 1617), II, i. Mermaid Series edition of Heywood's works, p. 99.

[70] *Ibid.*, II, iii; pp. 103–104.   [72] *Ibid.*, II, iii; pp. 104–106.

[71] *Ibid.*, II, iii; p. 104.   [73] *Ibid.*, III, ii; p. 113.

guises of Shortyard and Falselight are not prepared for, nor, with one minor exception, is there any word or action to tell who these men are.[74] The Country Wench's Father makes no preliminary remarks about his disguise, enters in costume without identification,[75] and reveals himself only indirectly through later comments.[76] Quomodo, on the contrary, emphasizes his contemplated masquerade, though he does not say how he intends to clothe himself,[77] makes himself known to the audience through his asides and soliloquies,[78] and finally discards his borrowed robes while the audience looks on.[79]

Thus while the ways of handling disguise upon the Elizabethan stage are varied, they are obviously modifications of a few general principles, all of which are exemplified in the comic technique of George Chapman.

[74] Thomas Middleton, *Michaelmas Term* (1606?), II, iii, 356–411, 477–492; III, iii, 1–63; III, iv, 196–262. There is slight identification in III, iii, 19–21.

[75] *Ibid.*, III, i, 42–126.   [77] *Ibid.*, IV, i, 77–121.

[76] *Ibid.*, III, i, 295–307.   [78] *Ibid.*, IV, iv, 1–59; V, i, 61–117.

[79] *Ibid.*, V, i, 127–131.

CHAPTER IV

USE AND MODIFICATION OF CONVENTIONAL COMIC CHARACTERS

DOMESTIC FIGURES

CHAPMAN and his contemporaries took most of their comic personages from Latin, Italian, and earlier English comedy, and added from observation a few creatures representative of contemporary social types. Despite obvious attempts at individualization Elizabethan comic dramatists seldom were able to conceal the conventional nature of their dramatic characters.

That the Latin stage folk were mere puppets has been recognized by modern scholars, as indeed it was recognized by the classic dramatists themselves, and both ancient and modern catalogues of the mannikins have been prepared.[1] Either directly from Plautus and Terence, or, as happened more frequently, through the medium of intervening Italian comedy, these Latin types emerged upon the English stage.

In Chapman's comedies the only unmodified Latin[2] characters are Gostanzo and Marc. Antonio, harsh and indulgent fathers in *All Fools*, a play based largely upon three Teren-

---

[1] Cf. Tucker Brooke, *The Tudor Drama*, pp. 160, 164; Thomas Marc Parrott, *The Comedies of George Chapman*, p. 732; Karl von Reinhardstöttner, *Plautus: Spätere Bearbeitungen plautinischer Lustspiele*, p. 101; G. Kenneth G. Henry, "The Characters of Terence," *SP*, XII (1915), 93–96; and Gilbert Norwood, *The Art of Terence*, especially Chapters V, VII, and VIII.

[2] To illustrate the modification of a stock Latin puppet, in *The Widow's Tears* is found the sole prostitute in Chapman's comedies, Thomasin, who appears once, utters four inconsequential speeches, and

tian comedies.[3] These parents are differentiated much as are the prototypes in Terence's *Adelphi*, have practically the same experiences as do the Roman fathers, and are made to demonstrate approximately identical conclusions concerning the wisdom of exercising harshness in the rearing of sons. All in all Gostanzo and Antonio are pure Latin types.[4]

Gostanzo believes in the strict control of the parent over the child, in the vigorous repression of all inclination to revelry and merriment, in the superiority of the country over the city as a place to bring up children, and in the infallibility of his own judgment. Suspicious, sometimes politic, and often underhanded, he is grasping enough to covet the most advantageous marriage for his supposedly industrious and upright heir. So convinced is Gostanzo of the idiocy of Antonio's affectionate bearing toward his son that he browbeats his weaker neighbor, advising him to deal more firmly. This counsel Antonio ignores, largely because of the peculiarly tender, almost motherly love he feels for his child. Yet Antonio is not too dull to enjoy a practical joke at Gostanzo's expense, and he rather than the more vigorous, shrewder Gostanzo is justified in the end.[5] In certain Latin comedies—for example, Plautus' *Casina*—the *senex* exhibits a futile amorousness. This quality Chapman's Gostanzo likewise displays.[6]

The proclivity to senile love-making which was occasion-

---

then is kicked off the stage by Tharsalio. She is not the generous, cultured, esteemed courtesan of Latin comedy, but a contemporary English drab, and Tharsalio's attitude toward her is not that of a Roman gentleman, but that of an Englishman of Chapman's day. Medice, parasite in *The Gentleman Usher*, is Italianate, vicious, and despicable, not at all the hungry and clever but amoral *parasitus* of the classic stage.

[3] *Heautontimoroumenos*, *Adelphi*, and *Eunuchus*.

[4] For a detailed consideration of the resemblances between Chapman's play and the Terentian comedies see Parrott, *op cit.*, pp. 702–708.

[5] The two fathers are characterized in *All Fools*, I, i, 124–409; II, i, 1–191.

[6] In *All Fools*, IV, i, 96–101, Gostanzo confesses that he has attempted

ally present in the old men of Latin drama was so extensively developed in the derivative characters of Italian comedy that the fatuous and ludicrously unlucky Pantalone became a stock figure in both the *Commedia dell' arte* and the *Commedia erudita*. Avaricious, but willing to expend much of his wealth to secure gratification for his libertine ambition, sly, because generally he had a position to maintain, and convinced that he was still vigorously attractive, he readily indulged in degrading masquerades and entrusted his affairs of heart to a trickster. Entrepreneur, amoureuse, daughter, and daughter's lover devoted their energies to baffling the old satyr. Mixed with Pantalone's established covetousness and modifying or even replacing his last flickerings of sexual passion, there was sometimes a desire to beget an heir for his wealth.[7]

To describe the stereotyped Pantalone is to portray Chapman's Lorenzo, whom he borrowed quality for quality from Piccolomini's *Alessandro*[8] and used in his comedy *May-Day*. As explained in the preceding chapter, Lorenzo is a wealthy Senator who in his old age becomes enamored of the youthful Franceschina and, after sending her gifts by her lover Angelo, gains entrance to her home by disguising himself as a chimney-sweep.[9] While he is slipping into the trap prepared

---

to seduce Gratiana, his own daughter-in-law, though he does not, at the time, know of her marriage to his son.

[7] For the general characterization of Pantalone see Maurice Sand, *The History of the Harlequinade* (a translation of his *Masques et Bouffons*), II, 9; P. L. Duchartre, *The Italian Comedy* (a translation of his *La Comédie italienne*), pp. 179–185; Winifred Smith, *The Commedia dell' arte, passim*; and R. W. Bond, *Early Plays from the Italian*, pp. xxx–xxxi.

[8] Professor Parrott's summary of the Gostanzo-Brigida action, the source in *Alessandro* of Chapman's story of Lorenzo and Franceschina, shows how ingenuous was the Englishman's reliance upon the Italian dramatist at this point. Cf. Parrott, *op. cit.*, p. 733.

[9] Franceschina speaks of Lorenzo as " . . . a Magnifico of the city, and one of the Senate" (*May-Day*, II, i, 395–396); Lorenzo empha-

for him by Angelo and Franceschina, his own daughter is keeping a tryst with her lover, thus defeating Lorenzo's avaricious scheme of marrying her to a rich but imbecile old rustic.[10] Lorenzo is Chapman's only thoroughgoing Pantalone in love, though certain other characters in his comedies are Pantalones with headstrong daughters. Lasso in *The Gentleman Usher* is defied by his daughter Margaret. But the husband Lasso has chosen for her is not a ridiculous lover or a clown like Gasparo, Lorenzo's selection; Lasso's candidate is Duke Alphonso, unsuitable only because of his age and because of Margaret's attachment for his son Vincentio. Lasso has no love affair of his own; and although he does attempt to coerce Margaret into an expedient but distasteful marriage, he is no simpleton. Foyes, slightly sketched father of Martia in *An Humourous Day's Mirth*, suspects all men, but entrusts his daughter to the dunderpate Labesha and insists that she marry him. Alarmed at her adventure with the King, however, he swiftly consents to her union with her lover, Dowsecer.[11] Lemot characterizes Foyes as ". . . that same old Justice, as greedy of a stale proverb,"[12] a description which

sizes his own age, though he believes himself to be as hardy as ever (I, i, 1–21, 110–145; II, i, 427–428); his wealth is several times mentioned (I, i, 23–25; II, i, 359–374, 470). Lorenzo's first statement of his interest in Franceschina occurs in I, i, 1–59, and Angelo's induction into the affair begins with line 60. The details of the masquerade have been presented in the preceding chapter of this study. In keeping with the convention of the goatish Pantalone, Angelo deliberately whets Lorenzo's lasciviousness in II, i, 507–521.

[10] The clown Gasparo, whom Lorenzo has selected as his son-in-law, possesses some characteristics of the Pantalone, but belongs rather to the convention of the ridiculous lover, to be discussed later.

[11] In their respective plays the emphasis is upon Martia and Margaret rather than upon their fathers, who are completely inconsequential. The relation of the two young women to the stock Pantalone's daughter will be noted later.

[12] *An Humourous Day's Mirth*, viii, 223–224.

suggests that had his creator developed him more fully Foyes might well have become a Pantalone of the Polonius type.

When the Pantalone's wife is one of the persons of the play, she only causes him trouble; she is as young, as wayward, and as resourceful as is his daughter or his mistress. This old husband with the young wife has been called one of the "favourite subjects of Renaissance comedy."[13] Like the amorous Pantalone, the uxorious type is illustrated in Chapman's comedies by only one well-defined personage, Count Labervele, in *An Humourous Day's Mirth*. The Countess is a gay young Puritan whose piety disturbs her only at opportune moments; her religion is a pretense in which she seeks refuge when there is danger that her lasciviousness may become known.

Labervele is introduced to the audience while he is scattering jewels and "posies" in his wife's private walks, hoping by his gifts of trinkets and philosophic love poetry to reconcile Florilla to her disappointing fate as an energetic wife to a sterile old man.[14] The Count has composed his own verses because he is suspicious of the activities of everyone else.[15]

Yet later this ultra-careful old husband displays a most stupid and inconsistent, but traditionally correct, gullibility. At the time of his first appearance with his wife he is hypocritically urging her to spend more time in the company of other people, his argument being that it is not his sterility (which the Pantalone never recognizes) but her constant melancholy which makes her barren. The promptness with which Florilla accepts his explanation and his advice alarms

---

[13] Bond, *op. cit.*, p. xxx. This kind of Pantalone is recognized, also, by Duchartre and other scholars.

[14] *An Humourous Day's Mirth*, i, 13–36.

[15] Maurice Sand (*op. cit.*, II, 18) speaks of distrust of others, a quality which Labervele shares with Foyes, as a frequent trait of the Pantalone.

Labervele.[16] Nevertheless within a few moments he permits Lemot, whom he characterizes as an "imp of desolation," to tempt Florilla because the bouncing young Puritan dame insists that only through trial can her virtue be established.[17] Suspicious of his wife's restless appetite but unbelievably ignorant of her positive misconduct, the Count in the end merely asks forgiveness for his troublesome jealousy.[18]

Into this old man Chapman introduces an interesting variation. It has already been pointed out that frequently the conventional Pantalone has a daughter who, like Aemilia in *May-Day*, disregards her father's wishes in choosing her husband.[19] But Chapman, who is inclined to mingle the farcical and the romantic in his plots, gives to Labervele not a daughter bent toward intractable amorousness but a son possessed of a melancholy misogamy. In his relations with this young Dowsecer, moreover, the Count indulges in none of the fussy, impotent bluster of the stereotyped old father; on the contrary, although his tactics are strange he does display sufficient natural and realistic concern to win a mild respect from his audience. Thus in some of his domestic experiences Labervele is the ridiculous puppet, the unoriginal laughingstock, of Italian comedy; but in one scene he is an appealing, pitiable, somewhat realistic figure.[20]

[16] *An Humourous Day's Mirth*, iv, 1–86.

[17] *Ibid.*, iv, 87–245. The testing goes through the second and fatal stage in vi, 1–135.

[18] *Ibid.*, xiv, 138–156.

[19] As Duchartre says (*op. cit.*, p. 182): "If he happens to have any daughters, . . . they worry their old father enough to drive him out of his wits."

[20] *An Humourous Day's Mirth*, vii, 1–219. This scene, entirely out of harmony with the rest of the farce, is the only one in which Labervele escapes from the narrow limits of the convention. Chapman ends Scene vii with irresponsible revelry, and the liberated Dowsecer completes his slight action in a farcical mode. Cf. xiii, 94–104; xiv, 52–105.

The husbands whom the Pantalones attempted to impose upon their daughters were usually such unhappy choices that the audience was compelled to sympathize with the rebellious young women; for since the conventional alignment of characters demanded that the father and the preferred lover be opposed and outwitted by the daughter and her gallant, it was customary to represent the Pantalone's selection as thoroughly unappealing and woefully unintelligent, as a figure no less farcical than the father himself. Hence arose the tradition of the ridiculous lover. Age was frequently though not invariably an addition to his other handicaps, and he was often a rustic;[21] but the details by which he was constantly identified were his fatuity in conducting his courtship (often with much prompting from outside) and the disdain, sometimes merely scoffing and again frankly contemptuous or actively abusive, which he was compelled to endure from the lady. He was, of course, always unsuccessful.

Such a lover is Labesha, who in *An Humourous Day's Mirth* has the support of Foyes in his courtship of the latter's daughter, Martia. Old, and clownish in mind[22] if not in external fact, Labesha is a fit companion for Foyes, although Chapman does not state the specific attraction which has put him into the good graces of the Pantalone. At the moment of his presentation to Martia, Labesha reveals all the stupidity that could be imagined; void of all social sensitivity and at

[21] Professor O. J. Campbell ("*The Two Gentlemen of Verona* and Italian Comedy," *Studies in Shakespeare, Milton, and Donne*, by members of the English Department, University of Michigan, p. 55) asserts that regularly, in Italian comedy, there are "three rivals, two young men and one clown." Aside from Labesha and Dowsecer, Martia has, as lover, Colinet (cf. *An Humourous Day's Mirth*, ii, 68–70), though Chapman does nothing with Colinet's affection for Martia.

[22] Note, in addition to his constant crudity, the rural rather than the urban figures of speech elicited by Labesha to explain the term "bearing double" (*An Humourous Day's Mirth*, iii, 16–23).

first lacking in initiative, he soon takes his cue from the old
father's suggestions and pays court to Martia in gross fashion.
Notwithstanding his glaring mental incapacity, Labesha is the
one man to whose care Foyes will entrust his daughter.
Martia finally accepts his unwelcome protection as a means
of escaping from her father's home.[23] As soon as Labesha
meets the courtiers, however, he is easily disposed of, for he
is so overcome with their flattery that he forgets his charge
and leaves Martia to enjoy herself among the gay gentlemen
from whom he was expected to shield her.[24]

To this superficially Italianate character Chapman adds
qualities not associated with the ridiculous lover in the *Commedia dell' arte* and the *Commedia erudita*. He makes him
constantly hungry,[25] thus ascribing to him a trait of the parasite of Latin comedy. Moreover Labesha is a tattler.[26] But
most amusing of all his accretions is his pose of melancholy.
When Labesha learns that he is definitely out of Martia's
thoughts and that she is carousing with the King and his comrades, he refuses to appeal to the King, but assures his friends
that never again will they see him a carefree dandy about
town. Disappointed love will plunge him into a melancholy.[27]
Such an appearance he does attempt to maintain, for soon he
is upon the stage struggling to soliloquize as he has heard
the melancholy and scholarly Dowsecer do.[28] His attitudiniz-

---

[23] *An Humorous Day's Mirth*, iii, 1–54. Labesha declares (vii, 38) that
his title is Seigneur de Foulasa. He demonstrates his general social ineptitude especially in xiv, 207–213, 255–261. For illustrations of his ineffectual, bucolic wooing see, in addition to Scene iii, the following passages:
v, 45–48; vii, 242–245.

[24] *Ibid.*, v, 1–201. For further indication of his complacent doltishness see viii, 130–170.

[25] *Ibid.*, vii, 221–222; xii, 35–52.

[26] *Ibid.*, v, 11–14, 101, 145; viii, 318–320; xiv, 142–143.

[27] *Ibid.*, xi, 9–12.

[28] *Ibid.*, xii, 35–67. Dowsecer's soliloquy occurs in vii, 65–216. Labesha's monologue not only is a half-witted attempt to imitate the philos-

ing speedily collapses, however, when he stands before a table covered with food, even though when detected he makes an effort to reëstablish his melancholy mien.[29] Melancholy, either genuine or factitious, is not a dominant strain in characters found upon the Latin, Italian, or early English stage; but Elizabethan Englishmen appear to have been so fascinated by the mood that dramatists, romancers, sonneteers, and scientists depicted it with all its paraphernalia. The burlesque of melancholy in this eccentric personage is a contemporary English touch.

It should be added, to complete the history of Labesha, that he loses Martia without a sigh. At first inclined to splutter aimlessly and ineffectively, he subsides in a moment with the observation that he will marry her better, if he can get her.[30]

Two slightly drawn but comparable characters are Gasparo in *May-Day* and Rebus in *The Widow's Tears*. Gasparo is introduced as an old miser.[31] His boorish greed is perfectly evident when he refuses to place any confidence in Lorenzo's good will because the latter has not turned Aemilia's dowry over to him, although the suitor overlooks the fact that he has not yet met his future wife.[32] In order to accentuate the old fellow's avarice Chapman permits Lodovico to tell how Gasparo has risen to wealth by preying upon the needs of reckless young gentlemen.[33] This man's rustic origin is revealed in his first speech, "God gi' you god morrow, sir; God gi' you god

ophizing of the scholar Dowsecer, but, like many another incident in the minor action of an Elizabethan comedy, is a burlesque upon an episode or a situation within the major action.

[29] *Ibid.*, xii, 53–67.   [30] *Ibid.*, xiv, 157–171.

[31] In both the dramatis personae of *May-Day* and the stage directions preceding I, i, 162, Chapman describes Gasparo as "an old clown." Lorenzo calls him a "snudge" or miser (I, i, 163) and a "ripe fruit——I think I might have said rotten" (I, i, 171–172).

[32] *May-Day*, I, i, 172–182.   [33] *Ibid.*, II, i, 74–78.

morrow,"[34] in the agricultural metaphor in which Lorenzo compares him to fruit upon a tree,[35] and in Lodovico's description of Gasparo's uncouth peasant father.[36] It is Lodovico also who emphasizes the lover's age and his disagreeable physical characteristics.[37] The dramatist makes it obvious that it is Gasparo's wealth which has induced the Pantalone Lorenzo to select him as son-in-law, despite Aemilia's aversion to such a match.[38]

Gasparo's courtship of Aemilia is not developed. Compared to Lorenzo or Quintiliano he is a secondary figure, and after the earliest scenes he is out of character as often as he is true to form. As the action progresses there are only two instances in which Gasparo is a conventionalized ridiculous lover. When he learns of Lorenzo's disguise as chimney-sweep with the seduction of Franceschina as motive, the rustic becomes alarmed lest Aemilia inherit some of her father's adventurous spirit and so disgrace her husband.[39] Again during the last moments of the comedy, when Lorenzo determines that, since Gasparo's courtship of Aemilia has been quite half-hearted and Aurelio's has been ardent, he will award the prize to the young lover, Gasparo replies with the unconcern of a suitor who never was in love: "Faith, and Jove give 'em joy together for my part!"[40]

Rebus, equally supernumerary in his play, drops out of *The Widow's Tears* before the completion of the second act, and his part is not varied, as is that of Gasparo. Sponsored not by the father of his lady, the Countess Eudora, but by a distant potentate to whom he constantly refers as "his Altitude," he conducts a wholly unimpressive suit, which consists principally of his contention that Eudora is making a great mis-

[34] *May-Day*, I, i, 167–168. [37] *Ibid.*, II, i, 52–70.
[35] *Ibid.*, I, i, 169–172.   [38] *Ibid.*, I, i, 185–194; II, i, 52–56.
[36] *Ibid.*, II, i, 70–74.   [39] *Ibid.*, III, i, 74–86. [40] *Ibid.*, V, i, 327.

take in rejecting him, and which becomes still more ridiculous through the insistence of Rebus and his confederates that he is a man of wealth and distinction in his own country.[41] The Countess is consistently contemptuous. Rebus, however, is not to be aroused to a manly rage; he fails to react even to the abuse of his rival, the defiant and blustering Tharsalio, preferring to excuse his terrified inertia by declaring that the court of Eudora is not the place in which to fight.[42] Since Tharsalio is not so scrupulous about resorting to violence in the presence of the Countess, Rebus finally retreats before the attack of his irrepressible opponent and does not reappear.[43] This defeated suitor has none of the rusticity of the usual ridiculous lover, nor is he described as aged; he does not have the support of a Pantalone, nor does he resign the lady indifferently. Like the type figure, however, he at least pretends to possess wealth, he is clumsy and doltish in pressing his cause, and he is subjected to ridicule and even physical mistreatment. He is an incomplete rather than a modified portrait of the stock ridiculous lover.

Although Sir Giles Goosecap, in the play to which he has given his name, belongs in general to a different classification, some of his qualities suggest the ridiculous lover. He is somewhat advanced in years; at least upon one occasion he admits that he is troubled with rheum,[44] an affliction which the Elizabethans associated with age. Not a clown like Gasparo, he is nevertheless invariably confused in his thought,[45] he exhibits an insurmountable stupidity in his attempts to comprehend and express ideas,[46] his supposedly cultured spirit prefers things French to things English,[47] he reveals the depths of his

---

[41] *The Widow's Tears*, I, ii, 37–66.   [42] *Ibid.*, I, ii, 97–155.
[43] *Ibid.*, II, iv, 131–201.   [44] *Sir Giles Goosecap*, III, i, 25–27
[45] For example, *ibid.*, I, ii, 7–9; I, iii, 33–55.
[46] For example, *ibid.*, IV, ii, 46–66, 209–219.
[47] *Ibid.*, III, i, 34–41, 231–232.

artistic soul in his fancy needlework,[48] and he pours out his fervent devotion to his lady in a "sonnet" on English mastiffs and French pages.[49] Goosecap is sponsored not by a Pantalone but by Lord Tales, his slightly more intelligent cousin, who attempts to bring some reason into Sir Giles's foolish utterances.[50] Though this suitor is subjected to some practical joking,[51] yet, unlike the typical ridiculous lover, he is successful in his courtship.[52]

The young woman whom the ridiculous lover pursued, the Pantalone's daughter, was a spirited girl of good social position, the *Amorosa* of Italian comedy. Usually her affair with the gentleman of her choice was an illicit passion, gratified by means of the assistance of a pandering nursemaid or a male intriguer. Such parental objection as there was to the marriage of the lady and her lover practically always arose from the Pantalone's preference for the loutish suitor.[53] With the exception of Dowsecer and Martia in *An Humourous Day's Mirth*, all of Chapman's lovers succeed in their courtship by resorting to subterfuge. And of Chapman's love stories, all except those of Vincentio and Margaret in *The Gentleman Usher*, St. Anne and Eurione in *Monsieur D'Olive*, and Clarence and Eugenia in *Sir Giles Goosecap*, are clearly as sensual as is the usual Italian dramatic amour. In all cases the hero and heroine are of high social rank, and Gratiana in *All Fools* is the only woman objected to by a parent on the ground of poverty or low caste.

Not all of Chapman's heroines are daughters of the Pan-

---

[48] *Sir Giles Goosecap*, II, i, 302–325; V, i, 1–25.
[49] *Ibid.*, V, ii, 337–364.   [50] *Ibid.*, V, i, 8–19, 170–181.
[51] *Ibid.*, II, i, 219–240.   [52] *Ibid.*, V, ii, 334–369.
[53] See the comments on the lovers in the following books: Bond, *op. cit.*, pp. xxxviii–xxxix; and Winifred Smith, *op cit.*, p. 9. The changed social position of the Italian lady, as compared with that of her Latin predecessor, is noticeable.

talone. His representatives of that stock character are Martia in *An Humourous Day's Mirth*, Aemilia in *May-Day*, and Margaret in *The Gentleman Usher*. All three of these personages have old fathers who attempt to coerce them into unnatural and undesirable matches because of the material advantages to be gained; but the heroines conventionally have their own way.

When Martia appears for the first time she is not characterized at all, except that the plot situation of stupid parent and foolish lover places her in the traditional rôle of Pantalone's daughter.[54] Later she is a gay coquette and true to the type, pleased to find herself surrounded by a bevy of married men and bachelors, delighted to match wits with the best of them, and in every way more of a responsibility than her doltish suitor Labesha can manage.[55]

In the middle of the comedy, when Martia falls in love with Dowsecer, Chapman attempts to reveal the entire process in three brief, stagey sentences;[56] and as soon as the melancholy scholar retires to his quarters, Martia is eager to resume her dangerous pleasures.[57] In the last scene she is assigned to Dowsecer in the most perfunctory manner with neither party to the contract displaying any affection,[58] Martia's sole observation being a passive agreement to live a better life.[59] She is merely a puppet, constructed according to the pattern of the recklessly gay young woman who is carried away by the frivolities of a lively social group, wooden in her lack of emotion, but possessing somehow cleverness enough to select her own husband.

[54] *An Humourous Day's Mirth*, iii, 1–54.
[55] *Ibid.*, v, 1–201.
[56] *Ibid.*, vii, 89–90, 150, 217. Chapman assigns to Martia only six of the 262 lines in this scene.
[57] *Ibid.*, vii, 250–252; viii, 272–293; xi, 13–19.
[58] *Ibid.*, xiv, 94–104.   [59] *Ibid.*, xiv, 304–307.

Aemilia is even less individualized than is Martia. A stereotyped figure in a conventional plot,[60] she does what the narrative requires without becoming for a moment an appealing character. Commanded by her father Lorenzo to encourage the advances of Gasparo,[61] she prefers the much younger and more romantic Aurelio,[62] but because of her father's constant watchfulness she does not at first know how to meet her lover.[63] Inwardly bold, not making even the Italian heroine's usual pretense at protecting herself from her too ardent lover,[64] she does affect a certain coyness,[65] preferring to observe external social forms.[66] She has an opportunity to develop into an emotionally interesting person when Chapman constructs her unwillingness to marry Gasparo not primarily upon a physical attraction for a more lusty man, but upon the fact that she feels no love for Gasparo and so considers that wedlock with him would constitute prostitution,[67] and again when Chapman permits her to express some consideration for Lorenzo's claim upon her affection and obedience.[68] But the dramatist elects to confine Aemilia to her preëstablished limits. During the last act and a half she does not speak a line, though she is upon the stage for most of the closing scene. Even when she escapes from the lukewarm pursuit of Gasparo and receives her father's consent to wed Aurelio, Aemilia says nothing.[69]

Margaret, in *The Gentleman Usher*, is much more fully developed. She does not appear during the opening scene, but within it there occur several passages in which other per-

[60] Chapman made very little change in the intrigue love plot when he borrowed it from Piccolomini.

[61] *May-Day*, I, i, 163–194.

[62] *Ibid.*, I, i, 195; II, i, 151–154.

[63] *Ibid.*, II, i, 176–182.

[64] *Ibid.*, II, i, 159–224; III, iii, 1–91.

[65] *Ibid.*, I, i, 195

[66] *Ibid.*, IV, ii, 1–21.

[67] *Ibid.*, I, i, 185–194.

[68] *Ibid.*, IV, ii, 10–14.

[69] *Ibid.*, V, i, 316–327.

sons discuss her.[70] These early lines present her as the lady whom Duke Alphonso wishes to marry but who is the sweetheart of the Duke's son Vincentio. This complication in itself suggests that Margaret may be the Pantalone's daughter. When in the second scene both her fussy parent, Count Lasso, and her aunt, the unrefined Cortezza, urge her to accept Alphonso's offer of marriage, she becomes unquestionably identified with the type.[71] Her speech during this episode, however, is not that of a conventional giddy pleasure-seeker like Martia or Aemilia, but rather that of a courteous, dignified, sober, self-respecting lady,[72] and this impression of good judgment is strengthened by her brief remarks during the next few scenes.[73]

In an excellent letter-writing scene[74] Margaret displays her competence in managing so temperamental an envoy as Bassiolo; she is a coquette and still a woman whose appreciation of the ridiculous in Bassiolo's nature arises from her own balanced intelligence. This same sense of rectitude, here not offended but only amused by the messenger's absurdities, is manifest in the early part of a scene in which she and Vincentio perform their own marriage service.[75] In this impromptu ceremony, deeply emotional and beautifully lyrical, Margaret's expression of genuine love is convincing evidence of her natural, wholesome feelings and determined spirit.[76] When later her father threatens her for her coldness toward

[70] There are references to Margaret in *The Gentleman Usher*, I, i, 28–31, 73–77, 80–106. She first appears in I, ii, 37.

[71] *The Gentleman Usher*, I, ii, 37–48.

[72] *Ibid.*, I, ii, 119–128, 153–161.

[73] *Ibid.*, II, i, 181–189, 301–303; III, ii, 235–243, 310–311.

[74] *Ibid.*, III, ii, 312–529. In this scene Margaret, having previously decided to do so, writes a letter to Vincentio, but allows Bassiolo to believe that his presentation of the Prince's love has prevailed upon her.

[75] *Ibid.*, IV, ii, 94–120. [76] *Ibid.*, IV, ii, 123–182.

the Duke, and the frightened Bassiolo is on the verge of deserting her and Vincentio or perhaps even of betraying the love affair to Lasso, Margaret accepts her father's rebukes and warnings with cool dignity and terrifies the usher into submission.[77]

Imprisoned by Lasso and fearful that Vincentio may have been slain, Margaret turns to various methods of suicide, only to shrink from them all; and at last, aware that it is her beauty alone which has attracted the Duke, she mutilates her features so as to escape further misfortune.[78] Chapman makes an evident attempt to psychologize the episode; and indeed this study of Margaret in desperation, recoiling from self-slaughter and eventually preserving her life at the sacrifice of her beauty, is as effective as any dramatic action in all Chapman's comedies. When near the close of the play the heroine offers to release Vincentio from his marriage vow because of her self-inflicted disfigurement, she becomes much too sentimental;[79] but this display of her complete unselfishness is Chapman's final stroke in his effort to paint a portrait of a noble woman.

While, then, Martia and Aemilia are slightly sketched, unindividual, gay young women, Margaret takes on the contour of a personality because she is minutely characterized. Cast into a predicament very like theirs, she is much more active in accomplishing her designs. While the heroine of *An Humourous Day's Mirth* sports with the wildest revelers of the court and still somehow manages to marry Dowsecer, and while Aemilia arranges and maintains an illicit amour with Aurelio, Margaret overcomes many serious obstacles in order to bring a commendable love to its appropriate satisfaction. As she works out her own solution, Chapman reveals her

---

[77] *The Gentleman Usher*, IV, iv, 57–170.   [78] *Ibid.*, V, iii, 1–82.
[79] *Ibid.*, V, iv, 100–121.

character: she is courteous, dignified, serious, determined, resourceful, reasonable, and capable of discerning and laughing at the humorous aspects of her own experience.

Chapman never depicts thoroughly convincing emotion in his comedies. Though his heroes and heroines may deliver conventional laments or soul-blasting denunciations, not one of them can give natural, effective expression to sincere, healthy feeling. From the emotional point of view Chapman's comedies, in spite of the employment of all the usual lyric devices of the day—declarations of love, love exultations, and expressions of grief over disappointed love or other misfortunes—are noticeably cold. The lyrical passages are always theatrical, never deep and true. Even the persecuted love of Margaret and Vincentio, his closest approach to a representation of intense feeling, is not satisfying.

Nevertheless Margaret is easily Chapman's best study of a woman in love, and to her he has given emotions more realistic than those of any of his other comic heroines. Though somewhat overcolored, she is much less mawkishly sentimental than are his melancholy love characters, such as St. Anne, Clarence, and Marcellina. And despite her emotional limitations she is more completely endowed with ordinary human characteristics than are any of his other women. She is Chapman's best romantic heroine, the most carefully elaborated, the most complete, normal, and vital woman to be found in all his comedies.[80]

When the ladies were not sufficiently receptive to the advances of their lovers, the latter often relied upon the good

---

[80] Like his contemporaries, Chapman preferred a multiple love plot. And while many of his leading ladies were sketchily characterized, practically all his secondary women were even less convincing. In the minor amorous action Chapman's men as well as his women are, as a rule, distressingly colorless.

services of procuresses, who undertook to arouse the uninterested women to a sense of wasted opportunity. Latin comedy had among its stock figures the old procuress or *Lena*, a character so elevated by the Italian dramatists as to become the *Balia* or nursemaid. While her status was improved, her morals underwent little alteration, and she functioned in much the same manner as did her predecessor. This somewhat subdued but still licentious creature is common upon the English stage; she is seen perhaps at her best in Juliet's nurse.[81]

Chapman has a few of these nefarious women in his comedies. His most perfect representation of the Italian type of dissolute female attendant is Temperance in *May-Day*. A recognized bawd,[82] she is nevertheless the waiting woman to Lucretia, the ward of the Venetian gentleman, Honorio. Taking advantage of her position as attendant to further her profession, she does all she can to involve her lady in an illicit intrigue.[83] Her language is coarse, her enthusiasm for sex adventure is shameless, her sympathy is always with the aggressive male, and she has little patience with a reluctant woman. Repulsed in her efforts to arouse Lucretia's interest in her undertaking, Temperance resorts to stratagem and fraud instead of to subtilty; and though she is careful to pretend that she anticipates no harm to her mistress, she hesitates to aid the lover until he has paid her, and she does not at all mistake the young man's intentions.[84]

---

[81] On the evolution of the procuress into the nursemaid see Bond, *op. cit.*, p. xl. Her social position was modified in keeping with the improved social position of her mistress, and practical shrewdness impelled her to exercise some caution in her activities. Duchartre (*op. cit.*, p. 285), unlike certain other scholars, maintains that the procuress continued in the *Commedia dell' arte*, as well as in the *Commedia erudita*, under the name La Ruffiana.

[82] *May-Day*, III, iii, 153–167.   [83] *Ibid.*, II, i, 1–34.

[84] *Ibid.*, II, i, 225–300.

Ero, attendant upon Cynthia in *The Widow's Tears*, is a less genuine *entremetteuse* than Temperance only because she has less freedom of operation. She has not the reputation that Temperance has earned; hence it may be assumed that her activity on behalf of Cynthia's lover is her first venture at pandering. Shut up in a tomb with her mistress to mourn the supposed death of Lysander, Ero welcomes the advent of the guardsman as a possible means of persuading Cynthia to return to normal life. Face to face with the prospect of starvation, she asks no pay for her services. Though Ero is not successful when first she encourages Cynthia to accept the advances of the soldier,[85] later she is able to awaken a ready response in her mistress, so that when the sentinel returns Cynthia is willing to eat and drink.[86] As soon as Cynthia breaks her vow of fasting she ceases resistance to her lover's solicitation.[87] Ero's work is done. She has not induced a young, unmarried woman to accept a lover, but has performed that service for an older woman who supposes herself a widow.

Arsace, recognized by all other persons as a bawd, appears in the same play. When the skeptic Tharsalio fails to make a favorable impression upon the young widow Eudora, he buys the help of Arsace who, by telling the Countess extravagant stories about Tharsalio's insatiable lust, arouses Eudora's latent sensuality and convinces her that Tharsalio is exactly the husband any widow must naturally desire.[88]

---

[85] *The Widow's Tears*, IV, ii, 19–183.
[86] *Ibid.*, IV, iii, 1–59. [87] *Ibid.*, IV, iii, 60–86.
[88] *Ibid.*, I, iii, 138–195; II, ii, 20–136. Arsace gains audience by pretending that because she is interested in Eudora's reputation she feels it her duty to warn her not to encourage the courtship of so lascivious a man. Perhaps it should be added to this discussion of the panderesses that conventionally the Italian functionary was successful.

CHAPTER V

USE AND MODIFICATION OF CONVENTIONAL COMIC CHARACTERS

DOMESTIC FIGURES (*Continued*)

MALE intriguers were employed in Italian and English comedy when the young lovers found it necessary to circumvent a Pantalone or other obstructionist parent. Midway between the panderess and the intriguer proper stands one of Chapman's characters, a character who suggests Pandarus in the Cressida story. He is Momford, uncle to Eugenia in *Sir Giles Goosecap*. When Momford learns that Clarence is in love with his niece, he urges the young man to dismiss all doubt from his mind, promising that he himself will prevail upon the Countess to accept the scholar.[1] Broad in his speech not only with the maid Winifred but also with Eugenia,[2] he relies not upon sensuality but upon curiosity to appeal to his niece, and thereafter successfully presents Clarence's cause.[3] He carries a letter from Clarence[4] and induces the Countess to read and answer it despite her feigned modest reticence.[5] Finally he arranges a meeting between the lovers, although in deference to the lady's wishes he promises that the scholar will not appear; and the rendezvous results in the marriage of the two young people.[6]

Momford has the way of a gentleman. He refuses to permit Clarence to feel that a difference in their rank means

---

[1] *Sir Giles Goosecap*, I, iv, 18–147.
[2] *Ibid.*, I, iv, 157–197; II, i, 17–43.   [3] *Ibid.*, II, i, 76–218.
[4] *Ibid.*, III, ii, 93–98; IV, i, 67–89.   [5] *Ibid.*, IV, i, 97–213.
[6] *Ibid.*, IV, i, 214–238; IV, iii, 82–97; V, ii, 51–291.

anything,[7] he wills all his possessions to his young protégé,[8] and he even manages to carry on his part of the Latin conversation with the scholarly Clarence and the scarcely less intellectual Eugenia.[9] He is no mere pander. He is an interested matchmaker; and whatever delight he may have in his own affairs of passion,[10] there is no suggestion that he attempts to promote one between Clarence and Eugenia. Socially gracious, he has a purely friendly interest in the matter, and so is not closely related to the coarse and mercenary old procurer.

In all comedy of intrigue much of the attention is devoted to the intriguer. In both the improvised and the academic comedy among the Italians the trickery was engineered by a servant, frequently the Harlequin or Arlecchino, as in Plautine and Terentian plays it was managed by the witty slave, or occasionally by the parasite.[11]

Arlecchino was a strange fusion of humor and pathos, of stupidity and wit. Although he was usually the servant of the young lover, he took no immediate interest in his master's slowly moving love affair until he was aroused by Colombine, the soubrette, servant to the lady beloved. Colombine was eager to see her mistress' desires fulfilled; hence she devised and initiated a plot, although in the foreground, carrying on the scheme as she directed, was Arlecchino, who was led to hope that if he could further the marriage of his master and Colombine's lady he himself might win the love of the soubrette.[12]

[7] *Ibid.*, I, iv, 19–35.   [8] *Ibid.*, V, ii, 295–300.
[9] *Ibid.*, I, iv, 140–141; II, i, 141, 142, 170, 171, 189, 190, 213–215, etc.
[10] *Ibid.*, II, i, 24–31, 62–66.
[11] Cf. Karl von Reinhardstöttner, *Plautus: Spätere Bearbeitungen plautinischer Lustspiele*, p. 101, and R. W. Bond, *Early Plays from the Italian*, p. xxxviii.
[12] Cf. O. J. Campbell, *The Comedies of Holberg*, p. 165; Winifred

A modification of this Italianate intriguer appears upon the Elizabethan stage, but in order to account for some of the characteristics exhibited by Chapman's tricksters it is necessary to revert to early native English drama and invoke the tradition of the Vice. This indigenous busybody, like other constantly reappearing stage personalities, underwent a marked development away from his original nature even while retaining most of his distinctive individuality. At first possibly a representation of evil tendencies in or about man, or perchance of the Devil himself, he emerged eventually as a character similar to the intriguing slave.[13] Recognized by

Smith, *The Commedia dell' arte*, pp. 9–10; P. L. Duchartre, *The Italian Comedy*, pp. 123–160; and Maurice Sand, *The History of the Harlequinade*, I, 57–101. There were other intriguers in Italian comedy, such as the sinister and dangerous Brighella (Duchartre, *op. cit.*, pp. 161–178); but Arlecchino was gay, stupid, and purely comic.

[13] See, for example, C. M. Gayley's "The Devil and the Vice," *Representative English Comedies*, I, xlvi–liv. Additional and not always harmonious discussions of the ancestry and characteristics of the Vice are to be found on pages 98–219 of Edouard Eckhardt's "Die lustige Person im älteren englischen Drama (bis 1642)," *Palaestra*, Vol. XVII (1902); in L. W. Cushman's "The Devil and the Vice in the English Dramatic Literature before Shakespeare," *Studien zur englischen Philologie*, Vol. VI (1900); in J. B. Moore's *The Comic and the Realistic in English Drama*, p. 65; in Wilhelm Creizenach's *The English Drama in the Age of Shakespeare*, p. 303; and in Felix E. Schelling's *Elizabethan Drama*, I, 53–54; as well as in the works of E. K. Chambers, Karl Young, and Wilhelm Swaboda, yet to be mentioned in this note. Professor Chambers, in a refutation of Professor Cushman's theory, asserts (*The Mediaeval Stage*, II, 204) that ". . . as a matter of fact, he [the Vice] comes into the interludes through the avenue of the farce . . . whatever the name may mean . . . the character of the vice is derived from that of the domestic fool or jester." Professor Young takes exception to the theory stated by Professor Swaboda in the expression "die Figur des Lustigmachers, des Vice der *Moralplays*" (Wilhelm Swaboda, *John Heywood als Dramatiker*, p. 60; quoted by Karl Young on page 120 of his article, "The Influence of French Farce upon the Plays of John Heywood," *Modern Philology*, Vol. II [1904]). Professor Young's contention is that a figure from the

critics as "the chief exponent of the burlesque element" in early English drama,[14] and blessed with much better intelligence than the Italian Arlecchino could boast,[15] he plunged into his undertakings with a verve and a good nature such as could arise only from delight in his own activity. Unlike Arlecchino, he took no orders from anyone; he could plan his own merriment. He reveled especially in any exposure of folly or weakness on the part of his victims; he had no ulterior motive, but acted because of his love of deviltry and because of his desire to promote satiric fun.[16]

Rinaldo and Lodovico, in *All Fools* and *May-Day*, are fairly close to the stock Italian intriguer. Because Rinaldo and his companions are aware of the harm that will result if Gostanzo learns that his son has married Gratiana, they have agreed that the fact must be concealed.[17] Despite this precaution Rinaldo, surprised by Gostanzo's abrupt question concerning the identity of Gratiana, speaks the first lie that comes into his mind; he declares that she is the secret wife of Marc. Antonio's son.[18] In other words there is thrust upon this young gallant, as upon the Italianate intriguer, a plot of deception and trickery which is not of his seeking and in which his

---

morality play cannot become a farcical figure, since ". . . in a pure farce no character is given a moral value" (*op. cit.*, p. 121), a condition quite the opposite of that found in the morality play. Robert Withington, in his article "The Development of the 'Vice'," in *Essays in Memory of Barrett Wendell*, pp. 155–167, assigns to the Vice a composite parentage: the devil of the miracle plays, the fool of the folk plays, the servant of the miracle plays, and the parasite of Latin comedy, modified by the influence of the Latin witty page. These references indicate the confusion and disagreement on the origin of the English character.

[14] Creizenach, *op. cit.*, p. 303.   [15] Schelling, *op. cit.*, I, 53–54.

[16] Professor Schelling (*op. cit.*, I, 79) points out that Merry Report, in Heywood's *The Play of the Wether*, "is a clever development of the Vice." Merry Report's qualities are essentially those here outlined.

[17] *All Fools*, I, i, 1–167.   [18] *Ibid.*, I, i, 169–186.

interest is at best secondary. But unlike the Arlecchino he has no incentive to persevere, he is not a servant but a nobleman's son, and he himself possesses the wit to carry on the plot once he finds himself involved.[19]

The plan which Rinaldo devises is simple. Gostanzo is made to accept his daughter-in-law into his home in the belief that he is helping Fortunio to escape the wrath of his father, Antonio. When the stern old man discovers that his son Valerio is in love with Gratiana, he decrees that the woman must leave his house immediately. Then Rinaldo suggests to Gostanzo that it would be an excellent jest to tell Antonio that she is the unwelcome daughter-in-law of Gostanzo, and to ask him to give her shelter until Valerio's father can be won to reason. Since Gostanzo is ever willing to belittle the good sense of his neighbor, he approves the plan and so it is arranged.[20] Rinaldo has the impudence and the energy of the conventional intriguer.

Lodovico, unlike Rinaldo, takes part in the intrigue of *May-Day* at the insistence of both lovers, and he definitely accepts and follows the suggestions of the lady who actually manages the intrigue.[21] Yet he is no servant; he is the nephew of the Senator Lorenzo and cousin to the lady Aemilia, whose instructions he follows in bringing her and her suitor together. Aemilia is directly interested in the meeting, not indirectly, as is the Colombine. The intrigue is sufficiently Italianate, however, for it consists principally of Aurelio's climbing a ladder to enter the chamber of his mistress.

One undertaking is not enough to keep this restless man occupied. He dabbles more or less in Angelo's plot against Lorenzo[22] and slips away upon a sly adventure of his own

---

[19] *All Fools*, I, ii, 85–147; II, i, 87–140.
[20] *Ibid.*, III, i, 13–113, 428–446.
[21] *May-Day*, I, i, 197–278; II, i, 110–224.
[22] *Ibid.*, III, i, 1–67, 142–249.

while Aurelio is making love to Aemilia.[23] This blind excursion places him in a most ridiculous position, because the lady to whom he makes advances is a young man in disguise.[24]

The activities of Angelo, roguish go-between for Lorenzo in his assault upon the virtue of Franceschina, have already been detailed in the discussion of disguise in *May-Day*. It remains only to repeat that since Angelo actually is a servant attached to Aurelio, he is clearly assisting his master's courtship of Aemilia by decoying the Pantalone away from his home; that the intrigue is forced upon him by Lorenzo; that although he confers with Franceschina about Lorenzo's visit to her, yet far from accepting her leadership, he flatly overrules her; and that since Franceschina is his mistress, his concern is suggestive of, but far from identical with, that of the typical Arlecchino. He has, finally, a feeling of amused superiority over his victim, an attitude which he shares with Lodovico and which is quite suggestive of the smart English Vice.

Another trickster in whom English and Italian qualities are combined is Valerio in *All Fools*. At first merely a boisterous gallant, he allows himself to be gulled into a foolish display of his foppish accomplishments and then sets out upon his course of deception in an effort to avenge the insult.[25] Vengeance sometimes prompted the trickery of the Italian Brighella[26] and Pedrolino,[27] though it would hardly seem necessary to find a stage tradition to account for a ubiquitous characteristic. When Valero begins his chicanery, he employs the methods of the Vice: he seeks out Cornelio's most assailable weakness, his unreasoning jealousy of his wife Gazetta, and arouses his victim to an extremely ridiculous exposure of that foible. Valerio is not content until Cornelio determines to

---

[23] *Ibid.*, III, iii, 148–179.   [24] *Ibid.*, IV, ii, 110–161; V, i, 169–232.
[25] *All Fools*, II, i, 367–428.   [26] Duchartre, *op. cit.*, p. 162.
[27] Sand, *op. cit.*, I, 201.

divorce his wife and in a duel strikes down one of her supposed paramours.[28] Were Valerio a true Vice, he would need
as provocation only the knowledge that Cornelio was suspicious of Gazetta's loyalty and he would be satisfied with a
ludicrous but harmless display of jealousy.

Gullers more strictly of the Vice type are Roderique and
Mugeron, inseparable courtiers in *Monsieur D'Olive*. They
have no reason for abusing the upstart D'Olive, except their
conviction that this "true map of a gull" is a victim constructed according to their own specifications. While D'Olive
is an unprecedented simpleton, his folly is amusing rather than
offensive; and although these young blades look down upon
him from their position of superior intelligence and greater
experience and pounce upon him as a conceited and aspiring
ninny, their scheme is not conceived in a spirit of animosity
and it is shaped by no feeling more vicious than a desire to pro-
vide general merriment at the expense of the butt.[29] Indeed
the entire D'Olive plot terminates in nothing but an exploita-
tion of his peccadillos. Introduced into the court by Roderique
and Mugeron and made an ambassador from the Duke to the
French King, the victim instantly loses any sense of propor-
tion he may ever have possessed and conducts himself as if
he were at least the equal of his master and the Duchess.[30] In
preparation for his journey to the King's court and his recep-
tion there he briskly assembles a tatterdemalion retinue,
though he has no wealth to maintain a display.[31] Just as he has
completed his arrangements events make his mission unnecessary. But the gullers, unwilling to accept a natural termination of their sport if artificial means can prolong it, send
D'Olive a letter which purports to be the Lady Hieronime's

---

[28] *All Fools*, III, i, 124–427.   [29] *Monsieur D'Olive*, I, i 260–420.
[30] *Ibid.*, II, ii, 1–341. D'Olive's sensible speech, lines 66–109, is
strangely out of character.   [31] *Ibid.*, III, ii, 1–201.

confession of love for him.[32] D'Olive satisfies their expectation for a short time before he discovers that this second fiasco, like the first, is the work of Roderique and Mugeron. Then his indignation is so outspokenly violent and so justifiable that the Duke once more takes him under his protection.[33]

The intriguer in *An Humourous Day's Mirth* is a gay courtier named Lemot. The play is a series of misadventures resulting from his machinations. Unlike most tricksters, Lemot does not limit himself to one victim. His interests are universal; the King and Queen of France, old Count Labervele and his young wife Florilla, old Countess Moren and her young husband, and the lady Martia are his principal victims, but his especial delight is Florilla, the factitious Puritan. All of Lemot's imposition is prompted by the love of mirth. There is not a single one of his dupes against whom he has any personal feeling; none of them has injured or even offended him, but all of them amuse him. He understands that the Queen, the Countess Moren, and Count Labervele are jealous of their mates, and that beneath her severely pious shell Florilla conceals a lascivious nature which only a superimposed Puritanism can keep respectable. To so crafty a mind as his, such half-submerged follies are a downright challenge. His entire nature demands that these people reveal themselves in public. His colossal impudence makes it impossible for him to discriminate between persons, and his shamelessness reaches its climax when he arranges a rendezvous between the King and Martia and then leads the Queen to the meeting, just to see what will happen.[34] With no moral or social earnestness about him, Lemot has no desire to correct the faults upon which he plays. Were he to remove them his

[32] *Ibid.*, IV, ii, 1–260.   [33] *Ibid.*, V, ii, 1–129.
[34] *An Humourous Day's Mirth*, vii, 23–33, 203–205; viii, 260–261; xi, 77–78.

cunning would defeat itself. As he often says, he must conse-
crate his days to mirth.[35] His hilarious, boisterous, noncorrec-
tive, good-natured, and nonpractical trickery is characteristic
of the English Vice, as contrasted with the sly, malicious, and
earnestly motivated scheming of Latin and Italian comic
intriguers.

Thus the tricksters in Chapman's comedies vary from the
modified Latin and Italian type represented in Rinaldo and
Lodovico, through a mixed species of which Angelo and
Valerio are examples, and into the conventional English Vice
illustrated by Roderique and Mugeron and Lemot.[36]

Gallants are ever present in Chapman's lighter dramas.
The type seems not to have been borrowed from foreign or
earlier native drama but to have come into existence upon the
stage because of the swarms of gallants that infested London.[37] Certainly Chapman is not alone among Elizabethan
dramatists in depicting these gentlemen. Every playwright
made constant use of them. And the writers of "Characters"
who recorded their impressions of English society a few years
after Chapman ceased to compose comedies[38] gave much attention to the gallants under one designation or another.
From these and other nondramatic sources as well as from
the comic dramas of Chapman and his contemporaries it is
clear that the gallant was an established literary convention.

[35] For example, *An Humourous Day's Mirth*, ii, 67.

[36] This statement of the variation in Chapman's intriguers does not
indicate a chronological development. There is no contiuous and consistent
modification of this figure in Chapman's comedies; the characters are here
grouped according to type, not date of creation.

[37] Professor Creizenach even extravagantly assumes that "it is evident
the poets in each instance drew their portrait from the life" (*op. cit.*,
p. 291).

[38] Chapman's last extant comedy, *The Widow's Tears*, appeared in
late 1605 or early 1606. Overbury's work was published in 1614, Butler's
(posthumously) in the same year, and Earle's in 1628.

The writers consistently present him as an irresponsible young man who swears many an eccentric, bouncing oath, who is gay to a fault, splendidly and fastidiously attired and strongly perfumed, and devoid of respect for persons and of reverence for institutions. He prefers to be known as "the stallion of the court," and yet is as ready for a slashing street brawl as for a graceful and dainty conquest. His love of excitement leads him to delight in games of chance and causes him to prefer, in his illicit amours, a jealous and watchful husband. Boastful of the favors he has received, he is an ingrained cynic on the subject of womanly virtue; he scoffs at love, considers the horn the natural consequence of wedlock, employs the bawd and the corruptible maidservant to effect his ends, and views marriage for himself favorably only when the prospective bride, regardless of her age, position, or other qualifications, possesses wealth. Contributing to his facility in subduing the ladies is his skill in dancing, singing, and playing upon the lute or the theorbo, and often his understanding of foreign tongues. Always a swaggerer and frequently a rogue, he keeps everyone in a turmoil with his smart chatter and his conceited dodges—everyone except the bailiffs, to whom occasionally he perforce surrenders and from whom sometimes he escapes by resorting to his shameless duplicity or his flashing sword.

Characters displaying these qualities in greater or less completeness appear in every one of Chapman's comedies. Dariotto, suspected lover of Gazetta in *All Fools*, is a gamester,[39] a perfumed debauchee who prefers a dangerous amour and boasts of his successes,[40] a fastidious and effeminate fop.[41] Valerio, in the same play, is vain because of his accomplishment as a guller;[42] when apprehended by an officer he resorts

[39] *All Fools*, II, i, 347–348.   [40] *Ibid.*, III, i, 270–372.
[41] *Ibid.*, V, ii, 5–22.   [42] *Ibid.*, II, i, 359–368; III, i, 124–129.

to violence and is hilariously triumphant when his reckless swordplay baffles the representatives of the law.[43] It is his unwarranted complacency over his ability to caper, sing, and play upon the theorbo that impels him into Cornelio's poorly concealed trap.[44] He is a gamester and a reveler whose guile alone prevents his father's detection of his debauchery and his ill-considered marriage;[45] and notwithstanding his fortunate birth he is so impecunious that Rinaldo easily believes Cornelio's statement that Valerio has been arrested for debt.[46]

In order to reveal Chapman's modification of a character as predetermined as the gallant, it is well to compare two intriguing gallants, Cleanthes from the earliest comedy, *The Blind Beggar of Alexandria*, and Tharsalio from the latest, *The Widow's Tears*. Both these men are confirmed scoffers. Cleanthes takes a grim delight in mocking Queen Aegiale's love for himself, and even induces her to kill her husband to further that love;[47] Tharsalio thinks that love is a myth and fidelity a lie.[48] Both are impetuous; Cleanthes fights his way through the Queen's guard to have audience with Aegiale,[49] Tharsalio routs Eudora's guard to pay court to her,[50] and both men silence their rivals by threatening violence.[51] They relish nothing so much as the seduction of a woman; Cleanthes therefore under different disguises marries two sisters and debauches his own wives.[52] Tharsalio, in an equally disgusting

---

[43] *All Fools*, II, i, 300–335.   [44] *Ibid.*, II, i, 369–422.
[45] *Ibid.*, I, i, 124–164, 219.
[46] *Ibid.*, V, i, 26–48. Cf. also II, i, 226–231.
[47] *The Blind Beggar of Alexandria*, vi, 21–64.
[48] *The Widow's Tears*, I, i, 100–148; I, iii, 93–98; III, i, 92–100.
[49] *The Blind Beggar of Alexandria*, vi, 9–19.
[50] *The Widow's Tears*, I, ii, 156–164; II, iv, 66–130, 265–277.
[51] *The Blind Beggar of Alexandria*, ii, 122–124. Cleanthes slays a rival in ix, 7–14. For Tharsalio's browbeating of his competitors for the lady's favor see *The Widow's Tears*, I, ii, 97–143; II, iv, 146–158, 179–205.   [52] *The Blind Beggar of Alexandria*, v, 75–145; vii, 24–93.

exhibition of impish ingenuity, wins the chaste Countess Eudora by employing the bawd Arsace to arouse her passion,[53] and he is frantic with ecstasy when, after a brief resistance, his sister-in-law yields to the soldier's entreaty and becomes his mistress.[54] Both of these men are intriguers; Cleanthes devises and directs all the trickery in his play, as Tharsalio plans and governs not only his own courtship of Eudora but also Lysander's trial of Cynthia's loyalty. Both have been injured by persons against whom they plot; the wife of Cleanthes has been killed by the amorous Queen Aegiale and the Duke himself has been exiled by Ptolemy,[55] while Tharsalio's comparatively minor grievance is the fact that Lysander has laughed at his failure to win Eudora and has irritated him with his confidence in Cynthia's repeated vows of loyalty.[56] Both men, finally, are ambitious; Cleanthes admits that he desires to occupy the throne of Egypt,[57] and Lysander openly states that he wishes to marry Eudora at least partly because her wealth will restore the fortunes of his decaying family.[58]

Cleanthes and Tharsalio have much in common, but there are wide dissimilarities between them. The former is essentially an Italianate character. His use of disguise to further his villainy is so extensive and so essential to the plot that

[53] The Widow's Tears, II, ii, 56–136.

[54] Ibid.,V, i, 22–80. Tharsalio planted the seed and nourished the swift growth of suspicion in the mind of his brother Lysander, Cynthia's husband.

[55] The Blind Beggar of Alexandria, i, 37–44.

[56] The Widow's Tears., I, i, 82–151; I, iii, 9–138.

[57] The Blind Beggar of Alexandria, i, 123. The bigamous marriages of Cleanthes are not, of course, steps toward his main object, that of attaining the throne; they are prompted only by lust (i, 235–240) and constitute an impediment which Cleanthes must cast off when he becomes king (x, 31–34).

[58] The Widow's Tears, I, i, 40–42; II, iii, 86–87; III, i, 49–50.

he appears to have borrowed his technique from the Arlecchino.[59] Cleanthes assumes four different personalities: Irus, the blind and pious beggar; Hermes, the choleric Count; Leon the usurer; and Duke Cleanthes. In these various characters he devotes his energies to a protracted career of polygamy, incest, robbery, murder, and treason. In one scene he plays the parts of three different men, disappearing from the stage as Leon the usurer, only to reappear a moment later as Count Hermes and swear to false statements on Leon's behalf; then, immediately after Hermes has left, Cleanthes enters once more in the guise of the hermit Irus and corroborates still further the perjured testimony he himself has twice given.[60]

On the other hand Tharsalio makes no use of disguise at any time, nor does he resort to underhand dealings. Rather he relies upon his interpretation of human nature. One of the superiorities of the later play over the earlier one is the dramatist's improved ability to present convincing reasons for the events which constitute his plot. *The Widow's Tears* proceeds consistently upon the basis of an extremely, painfully cynical philosophy of life, and every incident recorded in the Cynthia and Eudora action follows in harmony with Tharsalio's views of humanity. No woman is respectable, he postulates; therefore all one can expect is that a cold widow like Eudora will capitulate to the first man who sufficiently arouses

---

[59] "Arlequin had to be granted the opportunity of assuming numerous disguises and of satisfying his incorrigible appetite for roguery."—O. J. Campbell, *The Comedies of Holberg*, p. 143.

[60] *The Blind Beggar of Alexandria*, iv, 41–182. Winifred Smith writes, ". . . still more remarkable, he [Arlecchino] was able in his own person to play several parts, even on occasion simultaneously" (*The Commedia dell' arte*, pp. 12–13); and again (p. 39), "Scala's scenarios indicate that the Pedrolino, Burattino and Arlecchino of his company . . . slipped into a disguise and dropped it again in the winking of an eye."

her sexually. From the same point of view it is quite simple to foresee that a woman as fluent as Cynthia in her protestations of loyalty to her husband will succumb to the first tempter who enters her life. Early in the opening scene Tharsalio is represented as convinced of two major propositions which prompt all his activities and adequately explain them: the notion that Confidence rather than Fortune is man's chief goddess,[61] and the idea that chastity is woman's supreme boast and paramount deception.[62] Because he acts in perfect accord with his lucidly expressed hypothesis, Tharsalio is a more convincing stage figure than is Cleanthes. The latter states no theories; without any rationalistic foundation for his conduct he proceeds exactly as a type intriguing gallant may be expected to act if the playwright observe the dramatic convention. He need not be motivated because he is stereotyped.

Tharsalio works directly toward his objective. He follows the course of action which he is confident will subdue Eudora, and he torments Lysander into making a test which he believes will reveal to both Cynthia and her husband the weakness of women's vows. Cleanthes aims at the throne of Egypt; and though he finally gains the crown, yet in contrast to straightforward Tharsalio he has spent all the intervening time masquerading and perpetrating every conceivable variety of mischief, much of which is of no service in furthering his ambitions.[63] So far as Tharsalio, by working upon the

[61] *The Widow's Tears*, I, i, 1–14.

[62] *Ibid.*, I, i, 100–146.

[63] Duke Cleanthes, lover to Queen Aegiale but disguised as Count Hermes, persuades her to kill her husband (*The Blind Beggar of Alexandria*, vi, 9–88); and, in the same disguise, he himself kills Doricles, prospective heir to the throne, and pays court to Princess Aspasia (ix, 1–34). These deeds do not place him upon the throne, however, for Aegiale swiftly drops out of the play, and nothing comes of the wooing of Aspasia. The numerous disguises have little to do with his accession to the throne;

weaknesses of his victims, provokes them into bringing their half-hidden follies to light, he functions as does the English Vice; and to the degree that Cleanthes depends upon masking and sharp dealing, he imitates the Italian Arlecchino or, in his more vicious moods, the Brighella.

The principal advance which Chapman made in this pair of intriguing gallants lies in two facts: he gave Tharsalio an unmistakable and intelligible motivation, while he permitted Cleanthes to act conventionally but without evident and related motive; and he kept Tharsalio consistent to a purpose and so created a unified, finished character, while he allowed Cleanthes to drift about so irresponsibly that he became, instead of one person, four puppets, not one of them acceptable as a king in the making.

The wives in Chapman's comedies are easily divided into two main groups, the faithful and the unfaithful, with a minor division of shrews. Such a classification was one with which English drama was quite familiar. Dramatically the shrew was as old as Noah's wife in the religious plays; the patient wife was present, though undeveloped, in those Biblical dramas in which Joseph questioned the chastity of Mary and became reconciled to her only after angelic intervention had persuaded him of his error; and the disloyal wife assumes a prominent position in such early farces as John Heywood's *Johan Johan*. Outside of drama there were numerous literary tendencies which established the grouping of women here given—Chaucer, fabliaux, folktales, ballads, and so on.

The faithless wives of Elizabethan comedy, however, were no more completely English than they were purely Latin or Italian, for just as the native playwrights had pictured robust women who outwitted their husbands to estab-

principally they enable him to satisfy lust and amass a fortune. He is crowned because he has defended Egypt against her enemies.

lish unlawful relationships with clerics or scholars, so Latin dramatists had depicted courtesans and debauched women, and the Italian comic masters had delighted in risqué situations.

Among the women of Chapman's comedies four are clearly faithless: Franceschina, wife of Captain Quintiliano in *May-Day*; Florilla, backsliding Puritan spouse of old Count Labervele in *An Humourous Day's Mirth*; Cynthia, boastful but profligate wife of Lysander in *The Widow's Tears*; and Eudora, the chaste widow enticed from her single life by tales of Tharsalio's "beastlihood" in the same play.

Of these characters Franceschina, in a play adapted from the Italian, is the most Italianate. Her husband is a compound of the braggart captain and the guller. It is a tradition in both Latin and Italian comic drama that the *miles gloriosus* shall be confident of his power over women and shall constantly be made a laughingstock by them.[64] In Italian comedy especially the *Capitan* is "always in love and always unsuccessful."[65] If the braggart has a wife she is untrustworthy, and hence Franceschina is strictly true to custom when she accepts Angelo as her lover.[66]

Florilla is the stock young wife of the Pantalone. She, too, must be unchaste in order to remain within the convention. The fact that she is a Puritan making her first appearance upon the stage to the accompaniment of her own vaporous moral and religious musing[67] distinguishes her as English

[64] See Reinhardstöttner, *op. cit.*, p. 105.
[65] Smith, *op. cit.*, p. 8. Cf. O. J. Campbell, *"Love's Labour's Lost Re-studied," Studies in Shakespeare, Milton, and Donne*, by members of the English Department, University of Michigan, p. 32.
[66] That she is Angelo's mistress is clear from *May-Day*, II, i, 322–326, 338–341, 365–366. Franceschina's activities were outlined in the discussion of disguise in *May-Day*.
[67] *An Humourous Day's Mirth*, iv, 1–57.

and contemporary in her most individualizing quality. She is associated with the Elizabethan stage satire of Puritans and Puritanism. Urged by her husband, as much a hypocrite as she, to spend more time with other people, she accepts the advances of Lemot and plunges into a whirlpool of exciting adventure.[68] She actively invites seduction.[69] When after the carousal Lemot tells her that he has no regard for her and has toyed with her only for the joy of seducing a Puritan, she reverts to her former canting ways,[70] but she has gone so far that she cannot escape classification as an unfaithful wife.

Cynthia and Eudora are realistic rather than conventionalized figures, realistic in the sense that their action is motivated by comprehensible considerations and that the story of their downfall is not a giddy skit of intrigue so much as a fairly serious approach, though an entirely cynical one, to a study of the psychology of sex. Neither to the women nor to the play can the term "comic" be applied with any justice; and the term "farcical," which always satisfactorily represents a stereotyped character or plot, cannot be applied here at all. The play is earnest. If not an authentic record of the playwright's observation of specific persons, Cynthia and Eudora are at least an unmistakable exposition of a bitter theory concerning human nature.

In brief the story of these two women is as follows: Tharsalio, exasperated by Cynthia's protestations of everlasting fidelity to her husband, Tharsalio's brother Lysander, and by Lysander's wholehearted confidence in these vows, at length persuades Lysander to feign death and test his wife's sincerity. Cynthia accompanies what she supposes is her hus-

---

[68] The details of Florilla's defection were stated in the consideration of Laberveie as a Pantalone with a young wife.

[69] *An Humourous Day's Mirth*, iv, 135–245; vi, 1–135.

[70] *Ibid.*, xi, 20–77.

band's body to the tomb, where she shuts herself up, with Ero for companion, to fast until life ceases. But before matters reach a desperate state Lysander returns disguised as a soldier, tempts his own wife, and after a rebuff or two wins her so completely that she offers to rip open her husband's coffin and help to place his body upon a cross so that her lover may escape the penalty for negligence in guarding the corpse of a crucified convict. The defection of Cynthia is most gratifying to Tharsalio, who meanwhile has been further demonstrating the correctness of his opinion. The cold Eudora has for a time scorned his suit as well as that of other men, but at last the bawd Arsace has so interested the Countess in his virility that she consents to marry him.

Cynthia and Eudora are not women who carry on gayly with gilded courtiers or rapscallion tricksters. Their appetite is gross and fundamental. It is devoid of all dash and glitter; there is neither wit nor cleverness about it; in Cynthia's case it is associated with matters as basic as the need of food and drink. Yet both of these women apparently are perfectly sincere in their early attitude; they are simply victimized by a shrewd and scoffing imp who senses their weakness as accurately as the English Vice ever did and who insists that they be made to confess it. But Tharsalio's spirit is not buoyant; he is not content to raise the eyebrows and smirk; he sneers. And the women, as if they had absorbed some of the heaviness of Tharsalio's nature, are not light-hearted. Moreover they are not puppets who leave the observer unconcerned, and they have no idiotic husbands who deserve all the horns they may get.

Of Griseldas Chapman has no perfect example, but he has some approaches to the type. No wife or maiden in his comedies is subjected to persecution sufficiently intensive to necessitate summoning her utmost powers of patient endurance. In *The Gentleman Usher* Cynanche is eulogized in a most enthusiastic manner by her husband, Strozza,[71] but she has never been tested, has never been tried and proved as the Griselda must be. Margaret, beloved of Vincentio in the same play, does undergo some trial, for she is driven by her father, Count Lasso, and urged by Duke Alphonso to marry the latter. But she gains her consolation and her strength from her confidence in the love existing between herself and the Prince, and not from a detached, independent nobility of character. Nor when it is apparent that Vincentio is dead and that she will be forced to marry the Duke does she accept her fate with calm, Griselda-like Christian resignation. She is in a flutter, she contemplates suicide, and she finally destroys her own features in an attempt to make herself less desirable in the eyes of Duke Alphonso. Through all these experiences she reveals her loyalty to her husband, though she does not suffer at the hands of her husband as the Griselda must do.

Chapman did create two heroines who are victims of their husbands' brutality, the brutality in each case arising from jealousy, a passion in which this dramatist had at least the usual Elizabethan interest. The women are Gazetta in *All Fools* and Marcellina in *Monsieur D'Olive*. These characters, created six years apart, are presented in very different fashions.

Gazetta is a shadowy figure. During the entire play she receives only a minimum of characterization. So indistinct is she that it is impossible to be certain whether Chapman meant to portray her as a delinquent or as a maligned wife. In spite of the courtiers' spicy talk about her[72] she protests that she never has done her husband Cornelio any wrong.[73] On the

---

[71] *The Gentleman Usher*, IV, iii, 4–37.   [72] *All Fools*, III, i, 308–335.
[73] *Ibid.*, I, ii, 48–53; II, i, 232–271.

other hand, while there is in the comedy no speech or episode indicative of actual misconduct on her part, she is so indiscreet that as soon as she is freed from the danger of divorce she rejoins her gay companions at the tavern.[74]

The uncertainty concerning Gazetta's position is due largely to the fact that during her few appearances upon the stage she is most of the time silent. In the entire play she speaks only fifty-six lines, counting numerous half-line, almost monosyllabic replies as whole lines. Of this inconsequential body of comment half is devoted to non-characterizing exposition; at one point Gazetta uses twenty-seven lines to inform the audience of her husband's suspicions and of his consequent abuse of her.[75] Although she is present during the whole of a long episode in which Cornelio makes all preparation to divorce her[76] and again during all of a still longer scene developing out of the revelry in the taven,[77] she speaks only three short lines in the former instance and not a word in the latter.[78] Of the twenty-six lines not already accounted for, one is Gazetta's identification of her husband for the benefit of the audience at the time of his initial entry upon the stage,[79] and the other twenty-five are her denials of the charges made by Cornelio in private conversation.[80]

Gazetta's story has practically been told piecemeal in this study. Suspected by her husband, she protests her innocence. When Cornelio offends Valerio by gulling him, the latter retaliates by stirring up Cornelio's anger toward Dariotto, a

[74] *Ibid.*, V, ii, 1–333.   [76] *Ibid.*, IV, i, 227–358.
[75] *Ibid.*, I, ii, 1–5, 20–41.   [77] *Ibid.*, V, ii, 1–333.
[78] In many scenes of this comedy Chapman follows the Latin practice of keeping women mute upon the stage. Gratiana and Bellanora also are present in both these scenes; but during the divorce action Bellanora speaks only two lines, Gratiana none, while neither utters a word in the tavern scene. Chapman gives these three women a total of five lines in the first movement of 132 lines, and none in the final scene of 333 lines.
[79] *All Fools*, I, ii, 42.   [80] *Ibid.*, I, ii, 48–53; II, i, 232–271.

courtier of whom the husband already is jealous. After wounding the gallant in a duel, Cornelio is about to sign a petition for divorce when his nose suddenly falls a-bleeding, and he refuses to put his name to the paper. Gazetta repairs to the tavern, Gostanzo and others work upon the provincial husband's imbecility, and he finally declares that he never had any intention of divorcing his wife. Gazetta is, then, an ambiguous, impersonal entity in a farcical and uncertain plot. She never becomes interesting in her own right and seems to exist principally for the sake of the trite intrigue plot and because of the opportunity which she supplies for the exhibition of Cornelio's ridiculous frenzy. Obviously Gazetta, though accused and mistreated, has such questionable morality and reacts to her misfortune so recklessly that she cannot pose as a genuine Griselda.

Marcellina is a much more clearly defined dramatic character. Before Chapman shows her to his audience he carefully explains her relation to her husband and to the rest of the world and affords her an elaborate and lucid, even if primitively direct, characterization. And as the play progresses the lady develops and exhibits further qualities, so that finally she emerges as a tangible person.

In the first scene Vandome is returning to his native city after an absence of three years. Speaking at length of his Platonic mistress, Marcellina, he describes her as a woman noble in character as in birth, beautiful, modest in conduct, dignified, and intelligent in regulating her own action. Scarcely has he ended when her husband, Vaumont, tells of the domestic misfortunes which have overtaken him because of his unreasonable jealousy. Like Vandome, Vaumont is certain of Marcellina's purity; but in the past he has been suspicious, and as a result his wife has withdrawn from the world under a solemn vow, has excluded everyone except a few lady attendants, and has refused to become reconciled to Vaumont. From this narrative there emerges a more detailed personality; to all the splendid traits directly named by the two speakers there is added the impression that melancholia and sentimentality are dominant qualities in the mind of this offended saint.[81]

As the action progresses there is no reason to modify any of the first impressions of Marcellina. The melancholia especially is reëmphasized[82] and the supplementary qualities of taciturnity and loyalty to Vaumont are added. In the first of the three scenes in which Marcellina takes part she is engaged in conversation with her sister Eurione, who definitely takes the lead in the dialogue, with Marcellina's replies so brief as to be almost curt. The same directness and finality of speech characterize her orders to her servants and her remarks to Vandome.[83] There is a cold incisiveness about her, so that Vandome at one time justifiably refers to her as "ice."[84] Her action in this first scene is slight. When Eurione chatters about St. Anne, with whom she is falling in love, Marcellina responds in a half-hearted way; then, interrupted by the unexpected arrival of Vandome, who has forced his way into her presence despite her refusal to see him, she addresses a few brief and self-pitying sentences to him and retires.

Much later Marcellina is upon the stage a second time. Vandome, in order to draw her away from the chambers where she has gone into seclusion, comes late at night to give a false report of Vaumont's liaison with one of the ladies of the court, to state that the wayward husband has slandered both Marcellina and Eurione, and to declare that Vandome as sworn servant to Marcellina has no choice but to defend her good name with his sword.[85] During this long scene the

[81] *Monsieur D'Olive*, I, i, 8–133.
[82] *Ibid.*, II, i, 84–86; V, i, 69–71, 165.
[83] *Ibid.*, II, i, 19–89.
[84] *Ibid.*, V, i, 77.
[85] *Ibid.*, V, i, 65–253.

recluse is practically silent. At first she asks two or three anxious questions concerning her husband's welfare; later, when her sister waxes madly indignant at the slander Vaumont is reported to have heaped upon both women, Marcellina murmurs a few mild remonstrances; and finally, convinced that her husband is in serious danger from Vandome's sword, she breaks her vow and goes out into the streets to protect Vaumont.

Marcellina makes her final entry after twenty lines of the closing scene have been spoken. She is greeted by Vandome, who explains that he has lied about her husband in order to entice her into the world again. She makes no reply, and is mute throughout the rest of the scene.[86]

Thus though Marcellina does and says next to nothing, she is a much more developed character than is Gazetta. She becomes known almost entirely through remarks that are made about her, and practically all of this direct characterization is delivered before she comes onto the stage. When Chapman permits her to appear and to speak, he is careful to maintain the already created impression of a dignified, reserved, melancholy, supersensitive, determined, loyal woman. That is, she is actively revealed to the audience by Vaumont and Vandome, and her part is so passive that she does nothing to disturb the impression so established.

Chapman presents no elaborately expanded examples of shrews. Both the Queen and the Countess Moren in *An Humourous Day's Mirth* would have become just such persons had they been given opportunity to mature. Both of

[86] *Monsieur D'Olive*, V, ii, 21–129. Marcellina is upon the stage, in the course of these three scenes, while 369 lines are spoken. Her total number of lines, counting "Never!" and similar short expressions as lines, is 35. She is nearly as speechless as is Gazetta, and like that wife takes actually no part at all in episodes which vitally concern her though she, like Gazetta, is present.

them are uneasy about their philandering husbands; both pursue their errant spouses and berate them severely when they detect them at their clandestine pleasures. The Countess is much more the termagant than is the Queen, but she is no more persistent and feline in her watchfulness. Lemot the intriguer plays upon their jealous, shrewish natures as he will. Whenever Count Moren busies himself with Martia, Lemot prods the Countess, who always sputters. After Lemot has arranged a revel for the King, the Count, and Martia, he conducts both wives to it. He has made the Countess believe that Moren is engaged in an irregular alliance. The Queen has the same understanding about the King, and is warned by Lemot that His Majesty is in danger of violence from persons interested in Martia. The wives surprise and reprimand their mates, and then are so completely deceived by the transparent excuses offered by the men that they are in no better position than before to dominate the rakes.[87] Like all the other personages in this play, the two shrews are quite unsatisfactorily characterized; and like all the other action, their commotion is futile and their accomplishments are nugatory.

[87] The Queen and Countess plots are presented through scattered passages occurring chiefly in Scenes iv, v, ix, xi, xiii, xiv of *An Humourous Day's Mirth*, where they were interspersed with a considerable quantity of additional and equally farcical activity.

CHAPTER VI

USE AND MODIFICATION OF CONVENTIONAL COMIC CHARACTERS (*Continued*)

FIGURES FROM THE STREETS

AMONG the street types found upon the Elizabethan comic stage one of the most prominent is the braggart soldier. This character, at first an unworthy Roman in the drama of Plautus,[1] became in Italian comedy an Italian swashbuckler and then, because of the unpopularity of the Spanish oppressors in Italy, a Spanish braggart or frequently a mincing dandy.[2] The traditional captain boasted of his conquests, both military and amorous, but he insisted that after all he preferred the wars to love. In reality he was a preposterous coward, unsuccessful alike upon the field and in the boudoir. He was generally put to rout by Arlecchino or by some such unmilitary person. His chief function was to be outwitted and cuffed by other people.[3]

Into his first comedy, *The Blind Beggar of Alexandria*, Chapman introduces Bragadino, who is explained in the dramatis personae as "a Spaniard" and who identifies him-

---

[1] See Maurice Sand, *The History of the Harlequinade*, I, 137–142; R. W. Bond, *Early Plays from the Italian*, pp. xxvi–xxvii; Karl von Reinhardstöttner, *Plautus: Spätere Bearbeitungen plautinischer Lustspiele*, pp. 103–107; and Pierre L. Duchartre, *The Italian Comedy*, pp 225–227.

[2] Bond, *op. cit.*, pp. xxvi–xxvii; Winifred Smith, *The Commedia dell' arte*, p. 8; Duchartre, *op. cit.*, p. 229; O. J. Campbell, "*Love's Labour's Lost* Re-studied," *Studies in Shakespeare, Milton, and Donne*, by members of the English Department, University of Michigan, p. 32; and Sand, *op. cit.*, I, 143–144.

[3] Duchartre, *op. cit.*, pp. 225–227; Smith, *op. cit.*, p. 8.

self as "Signor Bragadino, the martial Spaniardo."[4] He has no importance, literally no part, in the comedy.[5] He is only the farcical butt for the more clever Cleanthes. When Elimine enters to keep her tryst with Cleanthes (here disguised as Count Hermes) the Spaniard follows her, expecting that she will prefer him to all other men, especially when she learns of his soldiership. So confident is he of success that he accepts the Duke's challenge to a wooing contest, but he suffers the captain's usual defeat. His bluster quickly subsides when his rival makes threats against his life; and this roaring, blood-thirsty boaster meekly follows Elimine and her suitor off the stage, walking backward and biting his thumbs in humiliation.[6]

Although Quintiliano in *May-Day* is much more versatile than is the stereotyped braggart, he displays many of the established traits. He is far more completely presented than is Bragadino. He possesses the expected complacency, thinking himself irresistible; yet he is betrayed by his wife, Franceschina. He likes to point out that he has had his way with a rather mean creature, the wife of his tailor;[7] but at the same time he is not promiscuously amorous, nor is either his

[4] *The Blind Beggar of Alexandria*, ii, 24.

[5] In the cutting which this comedy undoubtedly has undergone (cf. Parrott, *The Comedies of George Chapman*, pp. 673–674) the action and the character of Bragadino may possibly have suffered; though that is not likely, since the nature of the Bragadino-Cleanthes incident, the organization of the plot as a whole and the tenuous relation of this episode to it, and the traditional qualities of the braggart, all indicate that Chapman could have had no further use for the Spaniard. In this one appearance Bragadino does all such a character can do: boasts of his amorous and military powers, and retreats from his position.

[6] *The Blind Beggar of Alexandria*, ii, 20–138.

[7] *May-Day*, II, i, 580–598. Whenever the traditional braggart has any success in love, it is a woman of base rank or depraved morals—or both—who shows him favor. Cf. Campbell *op. cit.*, pp. 32–33.

boasting or his cowardice excessive. He varies from the norm further in that although he is apparently a soldier, talking about the wars and interested in gathering a company for some impending military operation, yet no one compels him, as the stereotyped soldier constantly is compelled, to exhibit either incompetency or terror. And he is not so slow-witted as is the usual captain; he displays a noteworthy ability in gulling.[8] This well-rounded character is carefully built up through frequent appearances, constant chatter, and incessant and varied activity.[9]

When Quintiliano is introduced he is the typical braggart captain expounding upon the necessity of his immediate departure to the wars, grandly assuming that his wife will be content just to know that he loves her, and glorying in the tears she is shedding over the imminent separation. Actually Franceschina is laughing behind her hand.[10] For a few moments after his wife has left the stage the soldier remains more or less in character, but soon he undergoes a transformation or enlargement. He becomes a trickster wily enough to induce the gull, Innocentio, to sell his property to finance Quintiliano's company. Then as soon as the troops are subsidized, Quintiliano forgoes his military interests and, becoming a gentleman of fashion, instructs his benefactor in the etiquette of the ordinary.[11] Within this scene Quintiliano is first a puppet captain, then an unprincipled and skillful cheat, and finally a gallant familiar with the gay society of the city.

During his second fling upon the stage Quintiliano again

[8] On Chapman's improvement of this personage, as compared with the prototype in *Alessandro*, see Parrott, *op cit.*, pp. 735–736.

[9] Quintiliano is upon the stage during the delivery of approximately eleven hundred lines, roughly forty per cent of the play; and he dominates all the speech and action contained in these eleven hundred lines. His part is the largest in the play, and his character is the most finished.

[10] *May-Day*, I, i, 279–303.   [11] *Ibid.*, I, i, 304–456.

begins conventionally, boasting of the hearts he has won.[12] Here he spends most of his time circumventing his creditors and, when he cannot entirely evade them, making part payment with money filched from the scholar Giovanello. Finally he returns to tavern revelry.[13] The same facets of his character are revealed, and in the same order, as in the previous scene.

When Quintiliano reappears, leading his band of merrymakers as any frivolous gentleman might do, he becomes aware of an amusing rivalry which has developed between his lieutenant Innocentio and his ancient Giovanello. Delighted with the quarrel and with Innocentio's challenge to his enemy, the captain so manages his subordinates that he develops the incident into an hilarious farce.[14]

Strangely enough, however, Chapman speedily forces this recalcitrant jester back into the narrow confines of the braggart soldier tradition. Still surrounded by the roysterers and fiddlers with whom he has been disporting at the tavern, Quintiliano suddenly begins to boast about the quality of his sword and about his skill in plying it. Innocentio conventionally makes it appear a poor weapon indeed, but the soldier is not perturbed. This shift to emphasis upon the traditional singularities of the captain appears to be a preparation for the incident which immediately follows. For now Quintiliano discovers Lorenzo disguised as Snail and hidden in Franceschina's coal room. The trite situation comes to the fore. The braggart's wife is untrue to him, the evidence is in his hands, but this sophisticated man about town, this rascal who has shown himself able to take care of his own interests, is sud-

---

[12] *Ibid.*, II, i, 583–598, 628–636. A slight inclination toward this kind of comment has already appeared in I, i, 308–309.

[13] *Ibid.*, II, i, 550–582, 599–627, 637–726.

[14] *Ibid.*, III, iii, 188–323.

denly bereft of all intelligence and cannot expose his wife and her lover, even though that lover be the incompetent Pantalone.[15] Having lost his wits temporarily (out of deference to custom), Quintiliano recovers them as soon as Franceschina withdraws. Indeed now he exhibits one of the rarest of all penetrative powers, the ability to be amused at his own shallow pose as a warrior; for in a simile protracted through sixty-four lines he compares the noble profession of fighting to the scarcely less commendable business of feeding.[16] But within a line or two his faculties again desert him and he relapses once more into the position of the impotent *miles gloriosus*, all because Franceschina enters in disguise, accompanied by her lover Angelo. Quintiliano realizes that he is viewing a vicious masquerade and makes amused, coarse remarks about this "doxy" and the pretty turn she is serving her unsuspecting husband, but he has no idea who she is.[17] Still deceived in the following scene, he does at length begin to sense the truth; and then he becomes proficient in managing the situation.[18]

Eventually Quintiliano dominates everyone. He inveigles Innocentio into paying court to a man disguised as a woman; he marries Innocentio to the bawd Temperance;[19] he has somehow learned the story of Franceschina's misdeeds and of Lorenzo's senile passion.[20] In disclosing his knowledge

---

[15] *May-Day*, IV, i, 1–99.

[16] *Ibid.*, IV, iii, 1–108. The simile is in lines 37–100.

[17] *Ibid.*, IV, iii, 109–133.

[18] *Ibid.*, IV, iv, 13–85. Quintiliano begins to understand in lines 72–85.

[19] This trick constitutes one of Quintiliano's most amusing deviations from the prescribed path of the braggart captain, because the bawd, customarily allotted to the warrior, is foisted off by him upon his victim.

[20] *Ibid.*, IV, ii, 238–245; V, i, 109–354.

of what has occurred he does not indulge in nonsensical bombast; he speaks mildly, like one who feels himself more than equal to the occasion.

Compared with Bragadino, Quintiliano is a much more detailed character study. Slipping automatically, mechanically, into the groove of the stage captain whenever his wife's intrigues demand that he do so, he is free at other times to reveal a versatile and altogether different personality. Blessed with something of Sir Toby Belch's love of a good gulling and with something of Sir John Falstaff's keenness in appreciating the grotesque humor of his own transparent pretenses, Quintiliano spends only his uninspired moments in the farcical, stultifying limbo of the puppet warrior.

Friends from the outside associated frequently with the inane Pantalones are the equally foolish pedants. Immersed in classical learning to the neglect of practical contemporary affairs, these misfits appear to have been suggested by Latin comedy rather than modeled upon it.[21] During the Renaissance this popular stage type developed as a satire upon the methods first of the medieval scholastics and later of the humanists as well.[22] Many of the pedants were schoolmasters, while others were doctors of medicine and of law.

Interlarding his conversation with quotations from Latin and, in the case of English representatives of the type, with Italian phrases, too; relying upon Latin tags to make the desired impression, especially during his unsuccessful wooing of a creature then probably hearing a foreign word for the first time; arguing in syllogistic formula; feverishly but unintelligently interested in his mother tongue, insisting upon

---

[21] For contradictory views concerning the direct borrowing of the pedant from Latin comedy see Bond, *op. cit.*, p. xxix, and Reinhardstöttner, *op. cit.*, p. 102.

[22] Campbell, *op. cit.*, pp. 36–37.

false etymologies, deriving mistaken pronunciations, and heaping up synonyms to demonstrate his acquaintance with the possibilities of the language, the pedantic schoolmaster becomes one of the truly ridiculous characters of the stage.[23]

Chapman's most obvious schoolmaster pedant is Sarpego in *The Gentleman Usher*. Designated "pedant" in the dramatis personae and so dubbed twice within the play,[24] Sarpego clearly is intended by his creator to represent the stock figure just described. He parades many of the usual qualities. That he is a schoolmaster there can be no doubt; Medice refers to him as one of "these scholastic wits"[25] and Sarpego calls himself schoolmaster in the introduction to a masque which he, the most intelligent person available, has composed.[26] He does not hesitate to apply the generic name to himself, nor does he falter in acknowledging his intellectual superiority. His contempt for the lesser wisdom of his associates is patent throughout his introductory speech. Writing down to his untutored audience, he assures them that the actors are not the persons they represent but are well-known comrades at the court, and generally gives evidence of the kind and degree of intelligence displayed by Bottom and his fellows under similar circumstances (though Bottom, of course, is by no means a pedant). In this same prologue Sarpego experiments with words, straining after synonyms with the hope of attaining an exactness and completeness of expression quite beyond the aspiration of ordinary men.[27]

Equally artificial is Sarpego's nearly invariable practice of speaking in rhymed couplets, a supposed refinement of expression in which no other character in the comedy indulges. These couplets are not the rhymes frequently used by Eliza-

---

[23] Campbell, *op. cit.*, pp. 36–40.   [25] *Ibid.*, I, i, 228.
[24] *The Gentleman Usher*, II, i, 191, 271.   [26] *Ibid.*, II, i, 196–201.
[27] *Ibid.*, II, i, 203–227.

bethan dramatists to lend dignity to the play, but constitute a glaring affectation.[28] The schoolmaster further adds to the impression of artificiality by making frequent use of alliteration[29] and by dragging his knowledge of Latin into his conversation. Not only does he use a passage from Plautus' *Curculio* to demonstrate his histrionic ability and his acquaintance with the literature of the ancient world;[30] he uses a Latinized vocabulary to express simple, mundane ideas that could be better and more easily stated in English. These classic words occur singly in Sarpego's utterances to persons of his own or superior rank, where they sound foolish enough;[31] but when the pedant addresses his inferiors his Latin and Latinate English descend upon the helpless, bewildered victims in overpowering and outrageous profusion.[32]

In preparing the masque the schoolmaster seizes the opportunity given him to huddle together almost every unnatural device known to conventionalized stage pedantry. He uses the argument from example and from classic incident to prove the dignity of brooms and the nobility of broom-men, and he employs the fallacious syllogism to demonstrate the identity of broom-men and philosophers. In heavy, labored, pedantic circumlocution he describes "green brooms, green rushes" as "verdant herbals, cleped broom," and "Dan Titan bright" as the one "Most clerkly call'd the scavenger of night." He toys with words, juggles with alliteration, and fills the air with synonyms.[33] Most of the standard parts for the assembling of a pedant schoolmaster are here.

The pedantic doctor of medicine is as well recognized and

[28] *Ibid.*, I, i, 163–227.   [29] For example, *ibid.*, I, i, 212–213, 227.
[30] *Ibid.*, I, i, 197–221.
[31] *Ibid.*, I, i, 226–227; I, ii, 17–18; II, i, 298–299.
[32] *Ibid.*, II, i, 125–128.
[33] *Ibid.*, II, i, 228–262. The masque is written by Sarpego, though of course he himself does not speak all the lines.

as frequent in comedy as is the schoolmaster.[34] Yet some of the stage doctors are admirably capable.[35] This phase of the tradition Chapman observed when he created Benevemus and Versey, physicians in *The Gentleman Usher* and *Sir Giles Goosecap*, both of them serious, conscientious, scholarly, capable men, not butts of merriment. Versey perhaps is more interested in the theory of his profession than comedy can well afford, but so is his patient, Clarence, and the effect is not farcical; and if Versey uses Latin somewhat freely in his conversation, he is at least matched by Clarence and Momford and Eugenia, and so escapes ridicule as a pedant.

In *All Fools*, however, Chapman displays the medical man in his folly. Doctor Pock, whose name alone is a jest, speaks no Latin, but he mouths his classically derived technical jargon with evident relish. He cannot view a simple scalp wound without indulging in an orgy of medical gibberish. He bargains before he undertakes the cure, and he compares the doctor to the lawyer (likewise ridiculed in this comedy) in that each can drag out the process of healing a breach or can bring a wound to a false cure so as to necessitate repeating the process from the beginning. Devoid of all integrity, this quack guarantees to suit the duration of recuperation to the plans of the patient and the prospect of fees.[36]

The notary in the same comedy is more strictly pedantic than is Doctor Pock, and he displays the foibles of his profession with equal distinctness. Like the doctor of medicine and the schoolmaster he prefers a mongrel vocabulary; he constantly inserts into his speech the Latin phraseology of the law courts and frequently expresses himself through a fusion of languages, as in "I have seen that tried in Butiro

---

[34] See Campbell, *op. cit.*, pp. 40–41; Bond, *op. cit.*, pp. xxviii–xxix; and Duchartre, *op. cit.*, pp. 196–207.

[35] Bond, *op. cit.*, pp. xxviii-xxix.   [36] *All Fools*, III, i, 373–425.

and Caseo, in Butler and Cason's case, *decimo sexto* of Duke Anonimo."[37] But by all odds his most self-satisfying moment arrives when he reads the bill of divorcement he has drawn for Cornelio. Exaggerating an attorney's elaborate repetition in order to exceed the best in exactness of diction, he emerges upon a prairie of synonyms and qualifications. This performance alone is enough to brand him an everlasting pedant.[38]

Another stock figure which occurs frequently in Elizabethan drama but of which Chapman's comedies afford a single example (the Governor in *The Widow's Tears*) is the stupid official, a character sometimes thought of as a semi-realistic satire upon rustic constables in Renaissance England, but more accurately recognized as a further addition to English humor from the Italian stage.[39] Filled with a sense of importance—the importance not of the task to be performed but of himself, who has to perform it—and yet lacking any comprehension of the manner in which he can best meet his responsibilities, he blunders about the stage, lost in a maze from which his addled wits cannot extricate him. He can neither understand nor use language; contradiction follows contradiction in his pompous declarations. Unworthy of respect as a person, he relies upon his authority to give him a monstrous dignity.

Chapman's Governor appears only in the last scene, but monopolizes the stage and prevents the dramatist from developing the dénouement of a much better action. As soon

---

[37] *Ibid.*, IV, i, 297–298.

[38] The notary episode occurs in IV, i, 227–358; the bill of divorcement begins with line 305. Professor Campbell (*op. cit.*, p. 40) mentions one pedantic character who sustains such a flight through forty-eight synonyms; Chapman's notary is content with thirty-one. He asserts, however, that he is presenting only a summary of the document, as "it would be something tedious to read all."

[39] Cf. Campbell, *op. cit.*, pp. 42–43.

as he arrives to assume his duties at his new post he is compelled to investigate the supposed murder of Lysander by
Lycus and the case of a sentinel, Lysander in disguise, who
has negligently permitted the theft of the body of a crucified malefactor. He does not see how Lycus can be convicted;
therefore he concludes it best to execute the defendant at
once. Swaggering and boasting, browbeating and domineering, this impostor tries impotently to do away with his felons.
When Eudora, widow of the former Governor, requests that
the accused Lycus be given a hearing before being led to the
slaughter, the fatuous potentate declares: "Therefore,
madam, set your heart at rest; I am seated in the throne of
justice, and I will do justice; I will not hear him."[40] But the
sudden revelation of facts connected with the mysterious case
overturns even his complacency, so that his last words are:
"I'll go with you. For my part, I am at a non-plus."[41]

The parasite was an older character descended from Latin
comedy by way of the Italian stage.[42] A flatterer and often a
trickster, he supported his patron's cause only in order to earn
an easy livelihood. Originally the parasite was a comic figure,
but Chapman's sole example of the type is a grim person, as
the parasite sometimes tends to be in Elizabethan comedy.[43]

Medice is a parasite in the court of Duke Alphonso in
The Gentleman Usher. The dramatist early describes him
as a penniless sycophant who notwithstanding his well-known
low birth, lack of breeding, and obvious parsimony, has somehow ingratiated himself with the Duke.[44] Alphonso's accept-

---

[40] *The Widow's Tears*, V, iii, 269–271.
[41] *Ibid.*, V, iii, 370. The Governor is present through lines 219–374.
[42] Bond, *op. cit.*, p. xxxviii; Campbell *op. cit.*, p. 42.
[43] Compare, for example, Ateuken, in Greene's *James the Fourth*.
Medice like Ateukin is called a fox by other persons.
[44] *The Gentleman Usher*, I, i, 106–127.

ance of Medice is so complete that he prefers him to his own son Vincentio, and in case of argument decides against the Prince.[45] As his position demands, the hanger-on is busy forwarding his master's activities, especially his suit to Margaret, with whom Vincentio also is in love. But Medice, turning from the mild cunning of the Latin and Italian parasites, resorts to violence, with the result that both Prince Vincentio and his friend Lord Strozza are nearly killed before Duke Alphonso learns to judge him correctly.[46] Not only does this parasite desert the tradition by preferring bloodshed to finesse; he departs further by keeping silent about his gnawing hunger.[47] So far as he wins and retains his place in the Duke's affections by fawning service, he acts like the stock parasite. Finally, as usually happens in Elizabethan comedy, his perfidy is revealed and he is beaten out of court.[48]

The lout or rustic, the clown whose nature and function suggest that he was in some way related to the loyal but stupid slave of Latin comedy, is another marionette giving indication of Italianate development, although in his migration to England he retained only half of his cinquecento characteristics. The Italian Pedrolino or Pierrot was an acrobatic, permanently rustic servant to the Pantalone. Because he was slow of wit he was the victim of the clever intriguers who induced him to assist, either unconsciously or unwillingly, in the trickery of his master's daughter and her lover. His dwarfed mentality led him to mistake words which he or others used, so that his remarks made little sense in them-

---

[45] *Ibid.*, I, i, 250–263.
[46] *Ibid.*, III, i, 1–13; III, ii, 302–303; IV, i, 1–8; V, i, 133–165; V, ii, 63–67.
[47] The half-starved parasite becomes less ravenous in English comedy. On this point see Gayley, *Representative English Comedies*, I, 101.
[48] *The Gentleman Usher*, V, iv, 182–282.

selves or else constituted inopportune replies to misunder-stood statements.[49]

Though none of Chapman's creations possess all the qual-ities of the typical lout, several of them belong to that classi-fication rather than any other. Among them, but neither the clearest illustration nor the most comic, is Bassiolo, major domo to Lord Lasso in *The Gentleman Usher*. Though Lasso is so subsidiary that he receives a minimum of characteriza-tion, his position in the plot is that of the Pantalone with a self-willed daughter whom he determines to marry to an unfitting older man. Conventionally Pedrolino is the servant of such a man, and generally he is influenced to aid the Panta-lone's daughter in circumventing her father, even though he is at heart faithful to his master.

That Bassiolo is a conscientious, qualified gentleman usher worthy of Lasso's confidence, there can be no doubt. Though he never displays much intelligence and lacks even average judgment, Chapman does not depict him as a rustic. He is a steward who knows his responsibility and takes it seriously.[50]

Not being provided with a witty servant or Arlecchino, the lover in this comedy, Prince Vincentio, himself gulls the Pedrolino, Bassiolo. His method is to insist that the usher treat him as an equal, not a superior, and accept his friendship on such terms. Bassiolo, elated, has some difficulty adjusting himself to the changed status, but so convinced is he of his

[49] Cf. Campbell, *op. cit.*, pp. 34–35, and *The Comedies of Holberg*, pp. 174–177; and Smith, *op cit.*, p. 72. Duchartre, *op. cit.*, pp. 251–261, lists only a few distinguishing qualities; and Sand, *op. cit.*, I, 183–234, gives a detailed account of the character, with an exposition of many traits not generally preserved in the representation of the English louts and con-sequently not recorded here.

[50] For example, *The Gentleman Usher*, I, ii, 1–29.

merits that he never suspects he is being manipulated.[51] He is to act as go-between for the Prince and Margaret. The heroine does her part, too, in practicing upon Bassiolo's conceit, particularly in a splendid letter-writing scene. She feigns unwillingness to accept a letter which he has brought from Vincentio. The usher insists, finally prevails, and then persuades her to dictate a reply, which he himself writes. Then as Bassiolo departs, feeling that he has done his friend good service, Margaret in a brief soliloquy asserts that she has done only what she wished to do.[52]

The dramatic purpose of this scene becomes clear when the usher, like the usual cowardly Pedrolino, fears detection and threatens to desert the lovers. With decisive promptness the lady assures him that if he reveal her secret she will disclose his part in the intrigue by inducing the Prince to show the letter written in Bassiolo's hand. The rebel at once subsides.[53]

In the same play Poggio is nephew to Lord Strozza, not a servant, and is gifted with certain loutish traits which Bassiolo lacks. He has one eccentricity of mind, one of speech, and one of function. His intelligence is so meager that he confuses his dreams with reality and declares that he refuses to waken until his dreams have come out right.[54] Just as confused in language, he regularly contradicts himself or brings in his modifying elements so late and so clumsily that a sentence makes two or three different impressions before it is completed.[55] Strozza calls him "Cousin Hysteron Proteron,"[56] and says of him: "He speaks huddles still."[57] His fantastic duty in the play is to bear tragic news ridiculously.

[51] *Ibid.*, III, ii, 97–121.
[52] *Ibid.*, III, ii, 312–529.
[55] For example, *ibid.*, I, i, 50–51; IV, ii, 211–223; V, ii, 71–75.
[56] *Ibid.*, I, i, 26.
[53] *Ibid.*, IV, iv, 95–153.
[54] *Ibid.*, I, i, 4–48.
[57] *Ibid.*, III, ii, 218.

This strange comedy is filled with sinister and near-tragic incidents, and it is Poggio who reports them. So constant is his activity as nuncio of disaster that other persons expect bad news when he appears and seldom are alarmed in vain.[58] The grotesque effect of doleful news in the mouth of this ninny is intensified by Poggio's incessant excitement, which causes him to rush frantically about the stage, displaying the physical agility expected of the Pedrolino but apparently indulging in none of the acrobatics of the Italian prototype. Unlike Bassiolo, Poggio is not involved in any intrigue and is not gulled.

Of the loutish attributes assigned to Sir Giles Goosecap, who has given his name to the play in which he appears, none is more delightful than his inability to understand his native tongue. He is even more perverse than Poggio in saying what no normal person could possibly mean. He requests that his cronies take a torch to see whether or not the moon is shining, saying that if it is he will presently consult his sundial.[59] He is willing to wager five hundred pounds on the distance between two cities, because he knows what it was when he was a boy; and "'Slid," he demands, "do not miles grow, think you, as well as other animals?"[60] He twists a well-known malapropism in a different direction, and asks whether caparisons be odious, to which query his comrades retort that they are odorous.[61]

Goosecap shares with Poggio the knack of contradicting himself. Just as Strozza asserts that Poggio "speaks huddles," so Rudesby declares to Goosecap: "I lay my life some crabfish has bitten thee by the tongue, thou speakest so backward still."[62] He is even more versatile in error than Poggio, for

[58] *The Gentleman Usher*, I, i, 130–131; IV, i, 4–5; IV, ii, 206–215; V, ii, 65–66.
[59] *Sir Giles Goosecap*, I, ii, 7–9. See also 102–107.
[60] *Ibid.*, I, iii, 33–55.   [61] *Ibid.*, IV, ii, 54–66.
[62] *Ibid.*, III, i, 18–20. For illustrations of the weakness see III, i, 24–28, 57–58; IV, ii, 109–110, 178–181.

he alone of the three louts can completely misinterpret perfectly clear statements. He mistakes "emphatical" for "fat"
and "nuptials" for "nutshells,"[63] as well as "comparisons"
for "caparisons" and "odious" for "odorous." And as if such
ineptitudes did not sufficiently establish his imbecility, he
finally questions which of two men is the older, "he or his
elder brother?"[64]

Unlike the other clowns, Goosecap is a ladies' man,[65]
though his reason for courting Penelope is his desire to take
the married men's part in a football game.[66] Besides he is
clever with needle and thread.[67] Frequently he adopts the
attitudes of his companions in a foolishly servile fashion, even
permitting his thoughtless imitation to lead him to decry
things English and praise things French and allowing his
mimicry of mere words to convert him into something little
better than a parrot.[68]

Bassiolo, Poggio, Goosecap, all three possess some of the
traits of the lout, but no one of them displays all the qualities. Bassiolo, the trustworthy but simple steward, is trapped
in an intrigue against his master and is frightened into contin-
uing his disloyal activity; but he is not rustic and he is not
an acrobat. Both Poggio and Goosecap have ceaseless difficulty with language, a difficulty which is only an external
indication of the fundamental obtuseness which is theirs.
Goosecap's troubles of this kind are much more varied than
are those of Poggio. The latter has a definite dramatic rôle,
that of a semiacrobatic bearer of bad tidings. Goosecap on the

---

[63] *Ibid.*, I, ii, 102–107; IV, ii, 215–219.   [64] *Ibid.*, V, i, 170–171.

[65] This point has already been considered in the discussion of the
ridiculous lover, and is mentioned here only for the sake of completeness.

[66] *Sir Giles Goosecap*, V, i, 78–84; V, ii, 368–369.

[67] This point also has already been presented.

[68] *Ibid.*, I, ii, 78–90; I, iii, 64–67; III, i, 34–38, 268–269; IV, ii,
28–31, 215–217.

other hand is an effeminate creature and a weak imitator of those whom he admires.

Among the contemporary social types immortalized upon the Elizabethan stage the pretenders or gulls were outstanding. Lacking birth or wealth or skill in foppery, these aspirants attached themselves, for training and advancement, to gentlemen whom they took to be successful gallants. Unaware that their natural uncouthness was enhanced rather than decreased by their efforts to inject themselves into a life for which they had no aptitude, they continued to inspire satiric mirth upon the stage long after the time of Queen Elizabeth.

Chapman's best gulls are Innocentio in *May-Day* and D'Olive in *Monsieur D'Olive*. The former selects Quintiliano as his model. As has already been explained, the captain induces his follower to sell all his property and place the proceeds to the warrior's account. In exchange Quintiliano makes Innocentio his lieutenant and promises to introduce him to the smart life of the ordinaries. This obligation the captain carries out, displaying the same spirit and emphasizing many of the same details as does Dekker in a comparable passage in *The Guls Horn-Booke*. First of all, says Quintiliano, one can get nowhere without fine clothes and plenty of impudence; aside from these qualifications "there's no prescription for gentility." This desirable arrogance will manifest itself in complete disregard for persons with whom the gull is not acquainted, and will be emphasized advantageously if he make every effort to eat just a little faster than anyone else, even though his companions at board be knights and justices, as Dekker has it. In conversation the prime requisite is a bellowing voice; what one says is of little moment. In order to avoid the disgrace of being mistaken for a poet or a scholar one must join in the games of chance after dinner.

Here the single warning is that one must stop before losing much money, for heavy loss "argues little wit at all times."[69] This advice Innocentio accepts in all seriousness.

How Lieutenant Innocentio becomes jealous of Ancient Giovanello and how Captain Quintiliano encourages the quarrel has already been outlined. In that episode Innocentio is an empty swaggerer and a coward, a less impressive Sir Andrew Aguecheek.[70] It has also been stated that Quintiliano tricks Innocentio into making love to a man disguised as a woman and finally marries him to a bawd.

From an analysis of Innocentio's part in *May-Day* it is evident that Quintiliano is the major factor in every scene in which the lieutenant's character is sketched. Chapman created this gull chiefly as a foil to his more important superior. The warrior's skill as a trickster is revealed principally in the discomfiture of Innocentio. Some of Quintiliano's best lines occur in scenes in which the lieutenant is present only to make openings for him,[71] and the captain's amusement at his own rôle is accentuated through his absurd imposition upon this convenient victim. Although Innocentio is unmistakably a gull, yet, since he takes his qualities from the demands of Quintiliano's character rather than from any independent claim which he might make upon the dramatist, he is painted only in the broad, unshaded colors of the puppet-like stock figure.

[69] Cf. *May-Day* (1601 or 1602), I, i, 380–449, and *The Guls Horn-Booke* (1608), Chapter 5: "How a Gallant should behave himselfe in an Ordinary."

[70] Although the slight resemblance between Innocentio and Sir Andrew must not be overemphasized, it is interesting to notice that just as Shakespeare's gull demonstrates his inability to understand the racy colloquialisms of Maria, so Innocentio exposes his colossal ineptitude for smart life when he fails to comprehend the figurative import of the warning that he "must carry no coals" (*May-Day*, I, i, 429–431).

[71] Such scenes are *ibid.*, IV, iii, 1–133; IV, iv, 13–27.

On the contrary Monsieur D'Olive exists by virtue of his own personality. In that part of the farce to which his story belongs he is easily the most important figure. Like all other gulls he aspires to become a consequential person at court. To that end he employs the only technique he knows, deliberate boldness. This intruder at once becomes a butt for the quick, experienced wits of the courtiers Roderique and Mugeron, who plot to make him entertain the court.[72] Yet D'Olive is not at all a stupid man. It is little commendation to declare that his intelligence is far superior to that of Innocentio, but it must be added that there are episodes in which Chapman sacrifices the consistency of this character apparently only in order to put certain sagacious speeches into someone's mouth. Consequently D'Olive is made a man who has observed life to some advantage. Upon the occasion of his first visit to the Duke he states that he has never before appeared at court because, having from a safe distance observed the swift and unforeseen rise and fall of persons already there, he has preferred a simpler life;[73] and when he witnesses the sentimental Count St. Anne's treatment of the body of the dead Countess he observes that a man generally appreciates his wife more after she has died.[74] Moralizing is not natural for the gull.

In spite of his frequent display of reasonably good sense D'Olive does not show to advantage in the company of the witty, dashing gentlemen of Philip's court, mainly because he has no ability at repartee. When Roderique and Mugeron begin to capitalize his eccentricity he drops back into the tra-

[72] *Monsieur D'Olive*, I, i, 393–420; IV, ii, 170–260.

[73] *Ibid.*, II, ii, 66–109.

[74] *Ibid.*, III, i, 64–69. Although the final lines are open to a cynical interpretation, the first two thirds of the passage are obviously intended to be taken soberly. In general, D'Olive is skeptical about women; see I, i, 340–358; III, ii, 121–124.

ditional position as definitely as does Quintiliano in the presence of Franceschina. He is never able to defend himself against their verbal thrusts; he can answer their pert, brutal sallies only with a grinning commendation of their cleverness.[75]

Too ambitious to be discouraged by his flagrant shortcomings, D'Olive attempts to replace tact with sheer effrontery.[76] So firmly is he convinced of his prerogatives as messenger of the Duke that he kisses the Duchess and upbraids her because she flies into a passion over his action, and his attitude toward Duke Philip in the same scene is that of one who admits no difference in rank.[77] He formulates the belief that when persons of unequal station are constrained to associate the only tenable relationship is one of intimate parity.[78] In accordance with this philosophy D'Olive curtly silences the Duke when the latter presumes to instruct him in the details of his mission to the French King;[79] and when his appointment is revoked and he has come to understand how shamelessly he has been abused by the courtiers, D'Olive assures Philip that the conduct of Roderique and Mugeron is a disgrace to any court and that the Duke cannot expect to win the respect of his people so long as he permits "such ulcers as these to gather head."[80]

In contrast to the thin and conventional Innocentio, D'Olive is an individual creation. At bottom he is undeniably a gull, for in addition to the fact that he is easy prey for Roderique and Mugeron he is called "gull" by both Roderique and the Duchess Jacqueline.[81] Yet there are moments when he quite violates the limits of the type, becomes a mor-

---

[75] For example, *ibid.*, I, i, 268–277, 373–375.
[76] *Ibid.*, I, i, 282–308.   [79] *Ibid.*, II, ii, 126–132.
[77] *Ibid.*, II, ii, 297–313.   [80] *Ibid.*, V, ii, 72–117.
[78] *Ibid.*, III, ii, 5–24.   [81] *Ibid.*, I, i, 393, 408; II, ii, 303.

dant philosopher and moralizer as cynical as any of Chapman's other men, or adopts a policy of bold aggression worthy of Tharsalio himself.

It is perfectly just to assert that Chapman's comic characters are largely representatives of types and seldom much more than puppets. In general they are semifarcical borrowings from the Latin, Italian, or early English stage, or occasionally from contemporary society and the contemporary English stage. They are comic figures with an wholly artificial existence and limited to the performance of perfunctory deeds. Some are even less, mere lifeless shadows which never attain to the feeble vitality of stock personages. Only a character or two in a play develops any robustness.[82]

Yet it is apparent that Chapman was interested in character. In the case of a few persons to each comedy he displays a decided improvement in characterization. Possibly as a result of increasing skill in writing, possibly as the result of a more serious endeavor to make his stage creatures lifelike, in his later comedies Chapman frequently did supply elaborate treatments of characters which had appeared in his earlier plays as slight sketches. By means of a catalogue of stock figures and by means of a comparison of representatives of types, this chapter and the two preceding ones have demonstrated not only that Chapman was generally confined to the

[82] Professor Parrott frankly states a similar point of view and attributes the fact largely to Chapman's tendency to clutter his stage with so many (often inconsequential) personages that he had little opportunity to develop even his important characters. See his *The Comedies of George Chapman*, p. 805. Professor Brander Matthews (*A Study of the Drama*, p. 245) discusses the tendency among Elizabethan dramatists to present unconvincing figures and to content themselves "with a bald daubing of character in the primary colors," which would seem to mean assigning a creature a few not particularly realistic qualities which would identify him as a type figure.

depiction of conventional stage characters but also that his late personages show a modification, a humanizing, a release from such strict confines of tradition as hampered his earlier creations.

There are two principal ways in which Chapman modified his characters. First, he often omitted some of the stock characteristics. Only one of the tricksters, Angelo in *May-Day*, is a servant, as the conventional comic intriguer was. In other words, although Chapman has persons who do the work of the Latin or the Italianate schemer, he assigns to them a different relationship to those in whose interest they execute their artifices. Ordinarily in his comedies they are friends, and the shift alters the tone of the play much as the elevation of the *lena* to the rank of *balia* altered the tone of the predecessor plays. Lodovico, intriguer in *May-Day*, is the only love-trickster who adheres to the Italian convention that the schemer shall be instructed by a woman.

A second method of variation is the attribution, to a character within one category, of qualities traditionally associated with another type figure. Chapman's Quintiliano in *May-Day* is an amalgam of the braggart captain with the typical guller; Florilla in *An Humourous Day's Mirth* is a compound of the Italianate wife of the Pantalone and the contemporary stage burlesque Puritan; Valerio, intriguer in the secondary action of *All Fools*, is a composite of the Italian Pedrolino, the early English Vice, and the contemporary English gallant.

Chapman's improvement in the characterization of type figures is due in general to his more complete representation of the persons depicted. In many instances the earlier personages are upon the stage very little, or (especially the women) are silent while they are present, or express themselves through words and deeds so unvaryingly conventional that no personality emerges. In the later comedies the characters considered are upon the stage more often and for greater periods of time, they take a more varied part in the action, and they are more carefully explained by the usual devices of the day, with the result that they are endowed not only with a few traditional attributes but also with a fairly large number of traits quite outside the convention. They have become more nearly complete.[83]

[83] An interesting aspect of Chapman's study of character is his frequent representation of two figures belonging to the same type in one comedy. In *The Blind Beggar of Alexandria* Cleanthes and Pego are both unscrupulous plotters. In *An Humourous Day's Mirth* there is the jealous old husband, Count Labervele, and the jealous old wife, the Countess Moren; and Florilla, Labervele's gay young wife, is paralleled not only by the gay young Count Moren, but also by Martia. In *All Fools* there are two tricksters, Rinaldo and Valerio, as well as the two contrasting fathers, Gostanzo and Antonio. *May-Day* has two ridiculous lovers, Lorenzo and Gasparo, and two principal gulls, Innocentio and Giovanello. Two noble and faithful women, Margaret and Cynanche, appear in *The Gentleman Usher*, as do also the two slightly subnormal comic figures, the dull-witted Poggio and the inebriate Cortezza. The characters in *Sir Giles Goosecap* travel in still larger groups: there are three ridiculous lovers, Goosecap, Foulweather, and Rudesby, three ladies, Eugenia, Penelope, and Hippolyta, and three pages, Jack, Will, and Bullaker. Chapman's only sentimental characters, the widower St. Anne and the abused wife Marcellina, are found in *Monsieur D'Olive*; and in this play there are two inseparable gullers, Roderique and Mugeron, and two pages, Pacque and Dicque. In *The Widow's Tears* Chapman pictures two women who boast of their chastity and yield to lover's entreaties, the widow Eudora and the apparent widow Cynthia, just as there are two professionally dissolute women, the bawd Arsace and the courtesan Thomasin. It is difficult to suppose that Chapman was unaware of this balance of characters.

CHAPTER VII
EMPLOYMENT OF ELIZABETHAN PSYCHOLOGY FOR PURPOSES OF CHARACTERIZATION

E LIZABETHAN stage figures were characterized largely in terms of sixteenth-century psychology, which was based upon an ancient system of physiology.[1] According to this old view man was a composite of mortal and immortal elements; his body and spirits were regarded as temporary, his soul as eternal.

A spirit was thought of as wholly physical, but so refined that Robert Burton described it as "a most subtle vapour."[2] All spirits operated to establish and maintain communication between soul and body and moved with remarkable celerity, "nothing in swiftness and nimbleness being comparable there-unto," wrote Timothy Bright, "Doctor of Phisicke."[3] Au-

[1] Detailed summaries of Elizabethan psychological theories may be found in Professor Edward Dowden's essay, "Elizabethan Psychology," *Essays: Modern and Elizabethan*, pp. 308–333; in Professor Murray W. Bundy's "Shakespeare and Elizabethan Psychology," *JEGP*, XXIII (1924), 516–549; and in Professor P. Ansell Robin's *The Old Physiology in English Literature*. More specialized applications of Elizabethan psychological theories to the drama of the period are Professor Elmer Edgar Stoll's Shakespeare criticisms, especially his "Shaksper, Marston, and the Malcontent Type," *MP*, III (1906), 281–303, and his two monographs, *Hamlet: an Historical and Comparative Study*, and *Othello: an Historical and Comparative Study*; Mary Isabelle O'Sullivan's "Hamlet and Dr. Timothy Bright," *PMLA*, XLI (1926), 667–679; and Ruth L. Anderson's *Elizabethan Psychology and Shakespeare's Plays*.

[2] Robert Burton, *The Anatomy of Melancholy*, I, 170. The edition referred to in this study is that of A. R. Shilleto, in three volumes.

[3] Timothy Bright, *A Treatise of Melancholy*, p. 43. The references

thorities agreed that spirits were distilled from the blood and that there were three distinct kinds, natural, vital, and animal, the classification being based upon differences in place of preparation, in degree of sublimation, in method of transmutation, and in function.

The grossest spirits, which resulted from the initial distillation, were the natural spirits, prepared in the liver. They moved through the blood in the veins and were associated with what Burton called "those natural actions,"[4] by which term he seems to have meant such processes as digestion, growth, and reproduction. Some natural spirits made their way to the left ventricle, where they underwent further sublimation. Thence they moved through the arteries, and they were called vital spirits because their activities were responsible for life itself. The climax of this orderly progress was reached when by further rarefication in the brain a portion of the vital spirits became animal. These spirits sped along the nerves to all parts of the body, giving "sense and motion"[5] to the physical organism.[6]

Man's soul likewise was regarded as threefold. The two lower levels of its activity were bound to the physical body and were not peculiar to man. It was understood that plants

are to the 1613 edition, to which is prefixed the 1586 "Epistle Dedicatory."

[4] *The Anatomy of Melancholy*, I, 170.

[5] The words "motion" and "to move" had internal as well as external significance. In addition to movements of organs, visible parts of the body, and the body as a whole, there were included in these terms impulses, desires, and passions.

[6] Dr. Thomas Vicary, *The Anatomie of the Bodie of Man*, p. 62, lines 2–4; p. 58, lines 9–14; p. 30, lines 4–12; and p. 59, lines 10–18. The references to the work of this old surgeon are based upon the edition of his *Anatomie* prepared for the Early English Text Society by Fredk. J. Furnivall and Percy Furnivall. Burton, *op. cit.*, I, 170, gives information identical with Vicary's.

and animals share with man the vegetal or vegetative soul and that animals share with him the sensible or sensitive soul, but that man alone is endowed with the rational or reasonable soul.[7] Each soul, or faculty of the soul,[8] was assigned its peculiar manifestation, the powers of the vegetative soul being assimilation, growth, and reproduction.[9]

The conception of the sensible or sensitive soul was much more complicated. It was assumed to be nobler than the vegetal soul and superior to it, possessing, in addition to the faculties of the vegetative soul, the power to know, to desire, and to move,[10] with the words "to move" interpreted in the larger Elizabethan sense. Robert Burton defines the *"sensible faculty"* as *"an act of an organical body, by which it lives, hath sense, appetite, judgement, breath, and motion,"*[11] and then classifies its powers under two captions, apprehending and moving.

According to Burton and others the apprehensive faculty had two manifestations, called "inward" and "outward apprehensive" powers, and was the equipment through which man could comprehend the qualities "of sensible things, present or absent, and retain them as wax doth the print of a seal."[12]

[7] F. N. Coeffeteau, *A Table of Humane Passions*, Preface (no pagination); Burton, *op. cit.*, I, 177.

[8] The language of the writers of the period leaves it uncertain whether they believed man possessed a triune soul or three souls, or possibly even four. When Burton, for example (*op. cit.*, I, 177), without comment mentions the theory of Paracelsus that the spirits constitute a fourth soul, he appears to be giving tacit credence to the theory of three distinct souls, although generally (e.g. *op. cit.*, I, 177–190) he speaks of the soul as one, but possessed of different faculties. Coeffeteau, on the other hand, quite consistently writes as if accepting the theory of several souls. See his Preface.

[9] Coeffeteau, *op. cit.*, Preface; Burton, *op. cit.*, I, 177.

[10] Coeffeteau, *op. cit.*, Preface.

[11] Burton, *op. cit.*, I, 179. Here, as in all other quotations in this study, the italics are those of the original author.

[12] *Ibid.*

The outer division of these powers consisted of the five physical senses under their present names, while the inner senses are listed as memory, phantasy, and common sense.[13] The term "memory" is self-explanatory and "phantasy" appears to be at least practically identical with the present word "imagination," the latter term or its equivalent, "imaginative faculty," being used in Elizabethan scientific writing to designate the ability to retain and, when called upon by the memory, to reproduce images of actual sense experience.[14] Common sense enabled one to interpret and evaluate the impressions gathered by the outward apprehensive faculties. Thus Burton maintains that it is not by his eye or his ear that he knows he sees or hears, but by his common sense;[15] and Coeffeteau asserts that the name is appropriate because to the common sense are brought the impressions of all the outward senses and because it compares and judges "formes" as "the particular sences cannot do."[16] In other words it is an intermediary between mere sensory contact and consciousness, be-

---

[13] Burton, *op. cit.*, I, 182; Coeffeteau, *op. cit.*, Preface; Vicary, *op. cit.*, p. 31, lines 8–28. According to Professor Dowden, there was sometimes recognized a fourth faculty of the sensible soul, reason. See his *Essays: Modern and Elizabethan*, p. 316, note 1. P. A. Robin, *The Old Physiology in English Literature*, follows Burton's phraseology. See his diagram on page 50.

[14] Coeffeteau (*op. cit.*, Preface) defines the "Imaginative sense" as "that wherein are graven the formes of things which are offered unto it by the *Common sence*, to the end the *Knowledge* may remaine after they are vanished away." Also after explaining how the common sense judges sense impressions, he writes: ". . . and then to preserve them [the sense impressions] in the absence of their objects, [the common sense] presents them to the Imagination, which having gathered them together, to the end she may represent them whensoever need shall require, she delivers them to the custody of the *Memory*; from whence retiring them when occasion requires, she propounds them unto the *Appetite*."

[15] Burton, *op. cit.*, I, 182. Robin, *op. cit.*, p. 167, refers to common sense as the "organ of perception."

[16] Coeffeteau, *op. cit.*, Preface.

tween what might be distinguished as the physical environment and awareness of it. It was regarded as the power through which one might interpret his experience with his surroundings.

On the foundation of the conception that all communication between the outward senses and the common sense was maintained by the spirits, there was constructed an ingenious explanation for sleep and dreams. Sleep was defined as inactivity of the outward senses and the common sense, induced by the inability of the vital spirits to travel between them. Vapors, arising from digestive processes or otherwise, mounted and clogged the nerves so that the animal spirits no longer could traverse them. The vital spirits then quickly took refuge in the heart; the common sense and the external senses, all commerce between them cut off, ceased to function; and the person slept. Of all the faculties phantasy and reason remained active; hence the sleeper dreamed. Gradually the fumes subsided or were dissipated, the spirits emerged from their hiding place and resumed their traffic, sense activity was restored, and the sleeper awoke.[17]

Just as the apprehensive powers of the sensible soul were divided into "inward" and "outward" faculties, so on the same basis the moving powers of the same soul were classified as appetite or internal motion and motion from place to place.[18] Appetite or internal motion was supposed to have two manifestations, the "concupiscible" and the "irascible." Both types of appetite were regarded as capable of desiring attractive objects and of shunning those which were unpleasant.

[17] Burton, *op. cit.*, I, 182–183; John Northbrooke, *A Treatise wherein Dicing, Dauncing, Vaine Playes, or Enterluds, with other idle Pastimes, &c., commonly vsed on the Sabboth Day, are reproued by the Authoritie of the Word of God and auntient Writers*, p. 38 in the edition prepared for the Shakespeare Society by John Payne Collier.

[18] Burton, *op. cit.*, I, 183.

But whereas the concupiscible appetite was mild, passive, and docile, the irascible was violent, active, and intractable—as Burton said, "... *quasi aversans per iram & odium.*"[19] According as internal motion was controlled by the concupiscible or the irascible power, it assumed the form of desire and impulse or of passion.

The highest point in human attributes was attained in the rational or reasonable soul, "... *by which a man lives, perceives, and understands, freely doing all things, and with election.*"[20] It possessed all the faculties of the two lower souls and in addition exercised distinctive functions.[21] Its peculiar attributes, organized as were those of the sensible soul but operative upon a nobler plane, were "the *understanding*, which is the *rational* power *apprehending*; the *will*, which is the *rational* power *moving.*"[22]

These latter are the qualities which were held to distinguish man from all other creatures. The understanding was supposed to enable him to arrive at logical conclusions based upon experience; and the power of dealing with generalities, instead of mere concrete sense impressions, bestowed upon him the ability to conceive ideas spontaneously, without dependence upon his sensory stimuli, and further enriched him with the supreme virtue, capacity to examine, reflect upon, and judge his own actions. The understanding, a moral and spiritual tribunal, freed man from the dominance of sense and released him from the tyranny of the present and immediate. Writers frequently referred to it as a guardian of the soul, just as they called the will the Queen or Prince of faculties.[23] The will was dependent upon the understand-

---

[19] Burton, *op. cit.*, I, 183–184.   [21] Coeffeteau, *op. cit.*, Preface.
[20] *Ibid.*, I, 188.   [22] Burton, *op. cit.*, I, 188.
[23] Bright (*op. cit.*, Epistle Dedicatory) speaks of reason as dwelling in a watchtower, and Coeffeteau (*op. cit.*, Preface) calls will the "*Queene of the powers of the soule.*"

ing; for will was accepted as an appetite and hence was regarded as blind.[24] Once will or rational appetite was advised
by the understanding, it compelled man to pursue that which
had been judged to be good and to avoid the evil, just as did
the sensible appetite operating within its proper sphere; but
will transcended and often ran contrary to the dictates of the
sensual appetite. Only in case of some weakness or malady of
organs, spirits, reason, or will was this control ignored, causing the lower ranges of man's nature to predominate.[25]

The conception of human action thus far outlined is
mechanistic and yet leaves room for the inclusion of factors
producing variation among men or within one man at different moments. Among the individualizing elements were the
humours extracted from the chyle,[26] *sanguis* or blood, *pituita*
or phlegm, *cholera* or bile, and *melancholia* or black bile.[27]
These fluids were supposed to determine disposition. Each
humour had its peculiar effect; according to Bright, the affections or feelings were first influenced, *sanguis* inducing
cheerfulness, *melancholia* sadness, choler anger, and phlegm
"heavinesse." The old doctor maintained that the mind was
equally affected, blood causing simplicity, black bile resulting
in "pertinacie" or pertinacity and careful deliberation, choler
producing rashness coupled with instability of purpose, and
phlegm leading to "flatte foolishnesse."[28] Such were the re-

---

[24] Burton, *op. cit.*, I, 190; Coeffeteau, *op. cit.*, Preface.

[25] Coeffeteau, *op. cit.*, Preface; Bright, *op. cit.*, p. 43. Appendix D of
this study contains Coeffeteau's résumé of the functioning of the human
machine under both normal and abnormal circumstances.

[26] Blood and phlegm were thought to be prepared in the liver, choler
in the gall, and black bile in the spleen.

[27] Some writers, among them Burton (*op. cit.*, I, 169–170), considered sweat and tears, hair and nails, to be "excrementious" or excrementi-
tious humours.

[28] Bright, *op. cit.*, p. 64.

sults when a single humour predominated; but the ideal state, called "temperament," was a perfect balance or equilibrium of the humours in which each performed its necessary service and yet all served as checks upon the others. Increasingly grave disturbances of this balance brought about eccentricity, illness, and even madness and death.[29]

Proceeding upon the basis of the scientific knowledge of his times, the Elizabethan dramatist attempted to present his stage creatures in terms which would be intelligible to his audience. To insist that the writers of comedy in the sixteenth century were especially skilled in the application of psychological conceptions to their personages would be uncircumspect, but to accuse Chapman and his fellows of ignorance of character or of lack of interest in it would be unjust.[30] Characterization by means of psychology was usually direct; in a few words a speaker revealed his own or some other character's disposition and told the audience in plain terms what was occurring within his own mind or within the mind of some other figure. Upon careful examination a passage which at first appears to be meaningless, or at best only a conventionalized figure of speech, is discovered to be a serious attempt at psychological character revelation. Chapman makes extensive use of physiological and psychological conceptions and terminology; and this chapter, without pretending to be a definitive study of his employment of such methods of

[29] Vicary, *op. cit.*, *passim*, especially pp. 69–70. For a detailed discussion of humours and health see Burton, *op. cit.*, in its entirety; for a synopsis see Robin, *op. cit.*, pp. 86–103.

[30] Undoubtedly the audience understood at least the general significance of such characterization, even though detailed and exact knowledge must have been limited to the professional and scholarly classes. Compare the state of the popular mind at the present time with regard to behaviorism, the Freudian theories, "complexes," and so forth.

characterization, presents a body of material sufficiently extensive to indicate the nature of his practices.

Love, either as unalleviated sensual desire or else as a more elevated attraction, is the nucleus of every one of Chapman's comedies. Love regarded as a physiological phenomenon was tremendously interesting to the Elizabethans. It was accepted as one of the passions, despite the notion that all passions were manifestations of abnormality.[31] "The heart," wrote Doctor Timothy Bright, "is the seat of life, and of affections, . . . of love."[32] And so it was generally understood; but by "affections" Bright meant feelings, and feelings might easily be converted into passions. Men in whom different humours predominated became passionate in different ways, and the Elizabethan explained the display of extreme "affection" not only in terms of strictly psychological displays but also largely in terms of the physical qualities of the humour dominant. The person whose excess humour was *sanguis* or blood was prone to fall in love. Blood was a hot, moist humour, and consequently the oversanguine man had heat and moisture above a normal degree. Hence the passionate lover has long been represented as weeping and sighing. Burton writes of the heat of love as driving tears from a lover's eyes like "drops from a Still,"[33] and explains that a breath or a sigh is a means of removing "the fumes of the heart" and thereby cooling it.[34] On a level with Burton's exposition of sighs is Coeffeteau's scientific statement that tears are produced by heat which arises to the brain of the person afflicted

---

[31] Coeffeteau, *op. cit.*, pp. 2, 18. On pages 32–35 Coeffeteau discusses eleven passions, one of which is love.

[32] Bright, *op. cit.*, p. 57. Also in the Epistle Dedicatory Bright speaks of the heart as "the seate of affection."

[33] Burton, *op. cit.*, III, 153–154.

[34] *Ibid.*, I, 175. All passions were supposed to cause excessive heat.

by love and there "causeth the humour to dissolve and discharge it selfe by the eyes."[35]

In harmony with this established conception of the effects of love, Chapman's Tharsalio draws attention to his display of the conventional characteristics of the suitor: "Only, madam, that the Aetna of my sighs and Nilus of my tears, poured forth in your presence, might witness to your honour the hot and moist affection of my heart."[36] Tharsalio, though a thoroughgoing cynic, a crafty wooer rather than a passionate one, knows how a genuine lover should perform and does not hesitate to apply the formula to himself.

With equal emphasis upon love as a humour Lodovico, who is nearly as emotionless as Tharsalio, declares that if any lady captivated his fancy he would "purge for her, for love is but a humour."[37] That troublesome humours could be eliminated by purging was accepted medical fact, for Burton suggests the use of such a method after phlebotomy and other methods have failed, but warns that the purge is a severe and dangerous remedy.[38] And with comic seriousness Lodovico affects to regard love as a desperate malady, to cure which the most extreme measures are justifiable.

Vandome likewise refers to love as a humour, and outlines the physical and mental changes which Eurione's apparently hopeless infatuation for St. Anne has wrought in her:

> Why, is it possible
> That you, whose frolic breast was ever fill'd
> With all the spirits of a mirthful lady,
> Should be with such a sorrow so transform'd?
> Your most sweet hand in touch of instruments
> Turn'd to pick straws, and fumble upon rushes?
> Your heavenly voice turn'd into heavy sighs,
> And your rare wit, too, in a manner tainted?[39]

---

[35] Coeffeteau, *op. cit.*, pp. 171–172. Coeffeteau discusses lover's sighs here, also. [36] *The Widow's Tears*. II, iv, 243–246. [37] *May-Day*, I, i, 238–241. [38] Burton, *op. cit.*, II, 275. [39] *Monsieur D'Olive*, II, i, 117–124.

Fumes generated by love melancholy have partially clogged the nerves through which the animal spirits should pass; consequently the vital spirits have retreated to the heart, so interfering with communication between the external senses and the common sense that the lady acts more or less like one moving in her sleep. All grace, happiness, and vivacity have departed; the entire sensible soul is affected and displays the usual changes which Coeffeteau associates with "heavines" and which he intimates may become fatal.[40] The fumes have risen to Eurione's brain too, "altering," as Burton warns may be the case, "the animal faculties."[41] Coeffeteau asserts that under the influence of love persons become quite altered mentally.[42]

Of two passages referring to Fortunio one mentions the conventional sighs and tears, as well as sleeplessness,[43] while the other agrees exactly with Coeffeteau in explaining tears as moisture forced through the eyes by hot vapors arising from the heart. This second passage next asserts that because of his love Valerio has undergone a noteworthy development of the "fruits of wit and virtue."[44] In other words love might have beneficent as well as deleterious effects, might sharpen as well as stultify the intellect. Such advantages usually resulted from successful or at least optimistic attachments. In the middle of a happy adventure Valerio becomes, as Burton

---

[40] Coeffeteau, *op. cit.*, pp. 332–333.   [41] Burton, *op. cit.*, I, 433

[42] "And that which is full of admiration, this Passion [love] doth so change & transform men, as it makes the wisest to commit great follies; it humbles the gravest to services unworthy of their rancke, it makes the most glorious to become humble and meeke, the covetous to be profuse and prodigall, and cowards to shew themselves hardy and valiant" (Coeffeteau, *op. cit.*, pp. 173–174). Compare the beneficent effects bestowed upon Valerio, immediately to be discussed.

[43] *All Fools*, I, i, 27–30.   [44] *Ibid.*, I, i, 7–14.

explains of many hopeful lovers, "spruce and keen, as a new-ground hatchet" and begins "to have a good opinion of his own feature, and good parts, now to be a gallant."[45] And he finally is outwitted through his eagerness to exhibit exactly those accomplishments of which Burton says every true lover boasts, his ability "to sing and dance, play upon some instrument or other."[46]

There are many references to the heat caused by passionate love and to the physical pain caused by any effort to repress the emotion. Bright says that passionate anger is relieved by expression, but that if it be not so relieved it will generate heat like "the scaulding of a boyling Chaldron not uncovered, or an hot Furnace closed up in all vents."[47] Any other passion would produce heat; but love was particularly likely to do so because it was caused by the hot, moist humour, as anger was caused by choler, the hot, dry humour. Melancholy was not an especially hot passion, since it was associated with a cold, dry humour. Yet it might be induced by love as well as by other causes. Coeffeteau asserts that if one who has died of *melancholia* be opened he will be found to have ". . . instead of a heart, . . . nothing but a drie skinne like to the leaves in Autumne."[48]

[45] Burton, *op. cit.*, III, 202.
[46] *Ibid.*, III, 203. Cf. *All Fools*, II, i, 367–420.
[47] Bright, *op. cit.*, p. 107. See Robin, *op. cit.*, p. 88, for a few quotations from Elizabethan literature expressing the same idea about passions. In a vein similar to Bright's, Lorenzo (*May-Day*, IV, ii, 57–58) reveals his secret experiences; aware that he should be infuriated by his detection of a lover in Aemilia's chamber, but unable, because of his old age—which Burton (*op. cit.*, I, 240) calls "cold and dry"—to feel any genuine indignation, he says: "I will conceal my rage a while that it may break forth in a fury."
[48] Coeffeteau, *op. cit.*, p. 333. Duchartre (*op. cit.*, p. 182) says the heart of the amorous, languishing Pantalone is "dry and shrivelled as a bit of orange peel" ("comme une pelotte de ficelle"—French edition, p. 183).

Angelo speaks mockingly to Franceschina of the loves of Lorenzo:

Lorenzo, Lorenzo, a gentleman of much antiquity, and one that for his love hath burned hundreds of hearts to powder; yet now it falls out that his tree of life is scorched and blasted with the flames of thy beauty, ready to wither eternally, unless it be speedily comforted with the sweet drops of thy nose.[49]

Valerio the gallant lover, begging his father to pardon a precipitate marriage, argues in the same fashion:

> . . . my heart had been consum'd
> T'a heap of ashes with the flames of love,
> Had it not sweetly been assuag'd and cool'd
> With the moist kisses of these sugar'd lips.[50]

And Fortunio at another point speaks of

> . . . my full love,
> Which but for vent would burn my entrails up.[51]

Less picturesquely but in a more ladylike manner Aemilia exclaims:

> Fie on this affection, it rageth with suppression.[52]

The Elizabethans held definite notions concerning the origin of love. Like all other feelings and passions this emotion was located in the heart.[53] Yet it was supposed to arise, in cases of ordinary attraction, within the liver, and in cases of holy love, within the brain. This discrimination between experiences leads Burton to segregate affection of appetite from affection of reason.[54] Bluntly discussing what Burton has called "Heroical" love, Bright says that the liver arouses

---

[49] *May-Day*, II, i, 372–377.   [51] *Ibid.*, III, i, 3–4.
[50] *All Fools*, IV, i, 143–146.   [52] *May-Day*, II, i, 151–152.
[53] Burton, *op. cit.*, I, 175; Bright, *op. cit.*, p. 57, and Epistle Dedicatory (no pagination).
[54] Burton, *op. cit.*, III, 18, 43.

not only appetite for food and drink but also "lust of propogation."[55] It is this unidealized conception of love between the sexes which dominates Chapman's comedies. When Tharsalio discovers that a soldier has seduced Cynthia, he takes from the cross a body which the soldier should have been guarding, and because the lover now is in danger of being nailed up to replace the corpse, he speaks of the theft as "a cooler to my venerean gentleman's hot liver."[56] The scholar Clarence admits that he is "all liver, and turned lover."[57]

Yet Clarence, like certain other characters in Chapman's comedies, prefers to think of his love as nobler than mere sex appetite. He calls it a spiritual attraction devoid of all passion.[58] In harmony with a theory expressed by Bright,[59] Clarence affirms that there is no passion in the soul (he means the rational soul) because the soul has no affections.[60] Momford repeats the assertion.[61] Dowsecer, also a scholar in love, says that his fancy for Martia has not changed his soul to sense but his sense to soul.[62] In other words a lover should regulate his life by the dictates of the reasonable soul, and Clarence has not permitted the appeals to his sensible soul to betray him into impulsive action. He has allowed the rational soul to dominate, with the result that any passion which may ever have characterized his admiration for his lady has been subdued to the understanding and the will.

In a different way the mastery of the reasonable over the sensitive soul is exemplified in comments subsequent to

[55] Bright, *op. cit.*, p. 58.   [56] *The Widow's Tears*, V, i, 71–77.
[57] *Sir Giles Goosecap*, I, iv, 83–84.   [58] *Ibid.*, III, ii, 24–25.
[59] Bright, *op. cit.*, pp. 2–3. Bright declares that the reasonable soul is void of passion because it is superior to man's physical nature; it has nothing to do with organs or changes in the body or its position, so far as such changes are indications of intense feeling.
[60] *Sir Giles Goosecap*, V, ii, 36–40.   [61] *Ibid.*, IV, i, 124–127.
[62] *An Humourous Day's Mirth*, vii, 213–214.

the attempt upon the life of Strozza. His problem is not to control rampant lusts but to endure the physical agony of his wound. To rage with the pain is to acquiesce in the dominance of the sensible soul, while to ignore the suffering is to assert the preëminence of the rational soul. In a long speech Lord Strozza says that although he knows his injury still shoots a distemper through his veins, yet by the exercise of patience he becomes all soul and is freed from the passions of his physical nature.[63] In corroboration his physician Benevemus observes:

> So is it plain, and happily approv'd
> In a right Christian precedent, confirming
> What a most sacred med'cine patience is,
> That with the high thirst of our soul's clear fire
> Exhausts corporeal humour and all pain,
> Casting our flesh off, while we it retain.[64]

Neither of these utterances is a mere pious figure of speech. Both men mean that Strozza has learned the essential fact of life, the practical consideration that his submission to the understanding and will, the qualities of the reasonable soul, makes it impossible for him to be swayed by the passions provoked by the distempered humours within his mutilated body. Although the physical conditions for passion are present, there is no fury because the highest faculties are functioning as they should. The clear, brilliant flame of the soul itself (which the classical peoples and those who adopted their physiology and psychology regarded as fire or temperature)[65] is intense enough to disperse the troublesome humours so that the pain and the passion cease. Fire, hot and dry, draws to itself or, as Benevemus says, attracts by its "high thirst" moist ingredients like vapors, fumes, and humours, and then by

[63] *The Gentleman Usher*, IV, iii, 43–52.
[64] *Ibid.*, V, ii, 8–13.   [65] Cf. Burton, *op. cit.*, I, 185.

virtue of its heat dispels them, cleansing the system and free-
ing it from disturbance.[66]

Profound grief was understood to be devitalizing. This
emotion as well as love or any other deep feeling might cause
tears when, as already explained, the heat which it produced
arose from the heart, distilled the humours of the brain,
and discharged them through the eyes. Lycus, telling how
Cynthia wept at the false report of Lysander's death, remarks: "Humanity broke loose from my heart and streamed
through mine eyes." To this confession the cynical and un-
sympathetic Tharsalio rejoins: "In prose, thou wept'st."[67]

When Valerio feigns passionate regret over his wayward-
ness in marrying without his father's consent he speaks of the
"tears, which so abundantly distil out of my inward eyes, . . .
being, indeed, as many drops of blood issuing from the creator
of my heart."[68] The "inward eyes" to which Valerio refers
are the inward senses or the inward apprehensive powers of
the sensitive soul, as distinguished from the outward apprehensive powers or five physical senses. The inward senses,
which were memory, phantasy, and common sense (and
sometimes judgment), resided in appropriate parts of the
brain[69] and were the powers through which one evaluated

[66] Both Strozza and Benevemus attribute the former's relief to his
"patience," a quality which, for the Elizabethan, practically always means
not merely mild, passive acceptance of conditions, but rather active
coöperation of man with his rational soul in enduring. Compare Shakespeare's use of the word in *King Lear* and elsewhere.

[67] *The Widow's Tears*, IV, i, 47–49.

[68] *All Fools*, IV, i, 85–90. Professor Parrott (*The Comedies of George
Chapman*, p. 720) rejects Collier's substitution of "crater" for "creator";
but the figure of the heart as a volcano erupting heat and vaporous blood
would be in harmony with Elizabethan physiology.

[69] Burton, *op. cit.*, I, 182. The memory was supposed to dwell in the
rear of the brain, the imagination in the forepart, and the common sense
and (when considered a separate faculty) the judgment in the central
portion.

experiences so far as one could evaluate without involving the rational soul. In other words, they were man's ability to see things as they are. Valerio means then that the heat of his passionate grief, rising from his heart to the regions occupied by memory, phantasy, and common sense, distils the vapours of his brain and causes him to weep. In addition he asserts that the process is so violent that his heart is emptying itself of blood and consequently of the vital spirits which take refuge in the heart during periods of distressing emotion; and unless this process can be terminated the blood and the vital spirits will soon be so completely expelled that death will be inevitable. Likewise the animal spirits which operate in the brain are in danger of being driven out or annihilated, for all spirits are mortal. The removal of the spirits from their usual channels causes not only sleep but also "syncope or swooning" and death.[70] Such excruciating agony attacks only the sensible soul, since it alone is capable of feeling and emotion. No such devastating passion is possible within the detached, equable rational soul.

A reference to the same physiological phenomenon occurs in a speech of Ptolemy's. After Count Hermes has murdered Prince Doricles, suitor to Princess Aspasia, the King gives voice to his grief, prefacing his lyrical lament with an explanation of his own inner experience:

[70] Cf. Burton, *op. cit.*, I, 170. Any extreme and unpleasant emotion, whether exciting or depressing, was considered dangerous. The death of Enobarbus (*Antony and Cleopatra*, IV, ix, 1–34), which may seem almost ridiculously unmotivated, is reasonably explained as resulting from the obstinate withdrawal of the vital spirits into their refuge within the heart under the enervating influence of grief and shame. It was largely because of the debilitating effect of sadness that a melancholy man was regarded as unhealthy, while men displaying other humours might be, except in extreme cases, merely amusing or, at most, annoying.

Oh, tell no more; instead of tears,
My beating heart dissolves in drops of blood,
And from mine eyes that stares upon this corse
Leaps out my soul, and on it I will die.[71]

In a similar fashion Eurione at one point remarks: "I shed not the tears of my brain, but the tears of my soul."[72]

When the human system was functioning correctly it was regulated by the reason. But the Elizabethans believed that reason might be so circumvented or obstructed in its operation that the human being began to act irresponsibly or, in extreme cases, madly. Bright says that if the brain is distempered or otherwise disturbed all commendable traits are obliterated and various kinds of "foolishnesse . . . dispossessing reason of her watch Tower" so modify human life as to force it into a state "far under the condition of bruit beastes."[73] Charron explains that there are two types of hindrance to wisdom. The first, which he calls "acquired" stupidity, is the result of prejudice against learning or of sheer pedantry in the exercise of it, and is not essentially physiological. The second impediment, "natural" stupidity, "proceedeth from the original temper and temperature" and terminates in one of two conditions: if the brain be too soft, moist, cold, and coarse, the result is sottishness; and if it be too hot and dry, the consequence is folly.[74] Vicary asserts that excessive moisture in the brain dissolves the vital spirits so that feebleness of both body and mind ensues and death follows sooner or later.[75]

In his activity man is constantly having sensory experi-

[71] *The Blind Beggar of Alexandria*, ix, 56–59.
[72] *Sir Giles Goosecap*, II, i, 156–157.
[73] Bright, *op. cit.*, Epistle Dedicatory.
[74] Pierre Charron, *De la Sagesse* (translated by Samson Lennard as *Of Wisdom* [London, 1670]), Preface (no pagination).
[75] Vicary, *op. cit.*, p. 33, line 32, to p. 34, line 2.

ences to which he reacts. Through his outward apprehensive faculties or physical senses he comes into contact with his environment, and every such contact arouses him. Through his inward apprehensive faculties, especially the common sense, he is made to regard the contact either as pleasant, profitable, and otherwise desirable, something to be prolonged or secured, or as unpleasant and undesirable, something to be avoided and shunned. The Elizabethan believed that as long as the attraction or repulsion is mild the concupiscible appetite alone is active. Only when the reaction is so violent that one intensely desires either to possess or to flee from the object, did the Elizabethan believe that the irascible appetite had become involved. Under normal circumstances both the concupiscible and the irascible appetites, as powers of the sensible soul, were subservient to the faculties of the reasonable soul, and except in purely routine matters no action occurred until the understanding had reported to the will and the will had directed whether the object should be seized or shunned. But sometimes the sensitive soul was so agitated or the powers of the reasonable soul were so hampered that the appetites of the sensible soul instigated action independently of the rational soul. Then it was that the reasonable soul was said to be hurled from its watchtower, and man in his conduct to descend to the level of "bruit beastes." Often a variation from the correct temperature or the correct consistency of the brain—or as Bright specifically states, the failure of the spirits to perform as they should[76]—was responsible for the breakdown of the system of control. Such variations within the brain might be constitutional and therefore permanent, or they

[76] Bright, *op. cit.*, p. 43. The sensible soul, functioning correctly, was entrusted with the power of acting independently in routine matters (Burton, *op. cit.*, I, 191), a purely practical concession which weakened the position of the rational soul in times of emergency.

might be purely momentary. A constantly hot and dry brain was conducive to impulsive, irrational action, because the agencies housed therein were rendered volatile, unsubstantial, and ineffectual. Conversely a perpetually cold and moist brain caused lethargy and torpor, because the agencies were mired and paralyzed. Temporary heat and cold, induced by unduly exciting and subduing emotions, had comparable transient effects.[77]

When Momford hears Eugenia's declaration that she weeps the tears of her soul, he promptly diagnoses her condition as one of temporary folly caused by the intense heat arising from a passionate love. He says: "Her sensual powers are up, i'faith! I have thrust her soul quite from her tribunal."[78] Because the higher powers have given way to the lower, she will act from impulse, not reason; she will satisfy the appetites of her sensible soul. Vandome has an exactly parallel situation in mind when he speaks of

> . . . the headstrong and incontinent vapours
> Of other ladies' bloods, enflamed with lust.[79]

A much more elaborate statement of the same principle occurs in a speech of Queen Aegiale. Count Hermes has advised the Queen, if she would induce Cleanthes to return to court, to uproot a magic plant, the destruction of which will cause the King's death. Determined to recover her paramour at the sacrifice of her husband, Aegiale explains her action on a purely physiological basis. According to her exposition of her own state of mind, passion so completely dominates her reason and her will that she cannot choose her course of conduct.

---

[77] Cf. Coeffeteau, *op. cit.*, Preface; Burton, *op. cit.*, I, 191; Charron, *op. cit.*, pp. 68–69.

[78] *Sir Giles Goosecap*, II, i, 160–161.

[79] *Monsieur D'Olive*, I, i, 89–90.

This serpent's counsel stings me to the heart,
Mounts to my brain, and binds my prince of sense,
My voluntary motion and my life,
Sitting itself triumphing in their thrones;
And that doth force my hand to take this knife,
That bows my knees and sets me by thy branch.[80]

Dastardly advice has aroused a passion in her heart, and the heat of that passion has deranged her brain. The understanding and as a consequence the will (to which all faculties of the sensible soul should be obedient, which alone should direct the activities of the body, and which in itself is an evidence of intelligent life, as contrasted with the life of the sensible soul, which is always beneath the conscious level) have been made useless. The passion usurps their authority and compels her, aware but like one under a spell, to commit the crime. As Bright declares, it is possible for a human being who is dominated by passion to act as if he had no rational soul at all. The Queen's understanding is drugged; the will, which is always forced to rely upon the understanding for guidance, is helpless; her sensitive appetites are in control. She acts like a brute.

Count Labervele, the jealous old husband, understands this kind of action. Thinking of his wife Florilla, whose Puritanism is obstrusive but not therefore more convincing, whose disappointment over her childless marriage is a source of uneasiness to her husband, and whose passionate nature he guesses, he muses:

But pure religion being but mental stuff,
And sense indeed all [careful] for itself,
['T]is to be doubted that when an object comes
Fit to her humour, she will intercept
Religious letters sent unto her mind,
And yield unto the motion of her blood.[81]

[80] *The Blind Beggar of Alexandria*, vi, 73–78.
[81] *An Humourous Day's Mirth*, i, 15–20.

Labervele frankly doubts whether it is normal that a young woman as robust as Florilla should fill her mind with pious love so completely as to exclude the allurements of physical passion.[82] He believes that the appetites of her sensible soul inevitably will be aroused, and that then she will hasten to satisfy the cravings of her physical nature without affording the rational soul any opportunity to check her impetuous action. He appears to expect that she will consciously refuse to permit her highest faculties to interfere whenever a human rival comes to woo her from her devotion to a cold, dull, impersonal ideal.

Florilla's later conduct justifies Labervele's estimate of her character. When the tempter Lemot begins to lure her into a life of abandon, she is coquettishly interested in the phenomena of her growing desires. Her lover, explaining her experiences to her, rightly emphasizes the activities of the sensitive soul and omits all mention of understanding and will. He tells her that his voice and his kisses, apprehended by the appropriate physical senses, arouse an appetite. This appetite is supported by the imagination, which presents the image of a situation which the purely physical common sense has sometime judged to be good and desirable. The appetite inflames the spirits of the blood, those natural spirits which, generated in the liver and carried through the veins, are involved in all rudimentary physical processes, including procreation. With imagination, appetite, and spirits active, with

---

[82] It was understood that spiritual love was capable of producing melancholy. (Part III, Section IV, of Burton's *The Anatomy of Melancholy* deals exclusively with "Religious Melancholy.") Perhaps a fear that Florilla may be developing such a malady explains Labervele's suggestion that a less contemplative, more social life may so improve her physical and mental health as to remove the curse of barrenness, for melancholy was thought to interfere with many fundamental bodily powers. If the Count had such a misgiving, it vanished swiftly.

understanding and will entirely shut out from participation, the sensitive soul is wholly enveloped in a blaze of passion.[83] Not all irrationality was supposed to be induced in the same manner. Sometimes the defect was regarded as the external manifestation of a disturbance within the composition of the brain itself. Such is the significance of Cynanche's analysis of the alteration observable in the speech of her wounded husband:

> Ay me, his talk is idle; and, I fear,
> Foretells his reasonable soul now leaves him.[84]

She judges that although Strozza's provocation is entirely different, he acts just as unreasonably, with as little oversight from the reasonable soul, as do Aegiale and Florilla. The physician Benevemus is in accord with the scientific beliefs of the day when he supplements Cynanche's observation with a statement of causes: "How want of rest distempers his light brain!"[85] Burton says that "waking overmuch . . . *causeth dryness of the brain, phrenzy, dotage.*"[86] The doctor supposes that pain from the wound has kept Strozza awake, and that this restlessness, in conjunction with the heat of the injury, has made his brain "hot, ardent, and dry,"[87] so that he yields to "unconsiderate judgement, simplicity, and foolishnesse."[88]

[83] "*Lemot*: . . . every kiss is made, as the voice is, by imagination and appetite, and as both those are presented to the ear in the voice, so are they to the silent spirits in our kisses.
"*Florilla*: To what spirits mean you?
"*Lemot*: To the spirits of our blood.
"*Florilla*: What if it do?
"*Lemot*: Why, then, my imagination and mine appetite working upon your ears in my voice, and upon your spirits in my kisses, piercing therein the more deeply, they give the stronger assault against your constancy."—*An Humourous Day's Mirth*, iv, 190–200.
[84] *The Gentleman Usher*, IV, iii, 82–83.
[85] *Ibid.*, IV, iii, 98.   [87] Charron, *op. cit.*, Preface.
[86] Burton, *op. cit.*, I, 287.   [88] Bright, *op. cit.*, Epistle Dedicatory.

Lycus is aware that heat injected suddenly into the brain may produce violent madness. Commenting to Tharsalio upon the evident effect of certain innuendos, he explains: "You had almost lifted his wit off the hinges. That spark jealousy, falling into his dry, melancholy brain, had well near set the whole house on fire."[89] Intense heat arising from a passion such as jealousy would transform a cold, dry, melancholy brain into one hot and dry or choleric. Expounding upon the effects of unhealthy or adust humours, Burton declares that they result in raging madness, such as Lycus must visualize when he speaks of wrenching Lysander's wit off its hinges.[90] Coeffeteau maintains that a furious anger, "by . . . inflaming choler, which by her naturall lightnes mounts up to the braine, may deprive man of the use of reason, & make him furious and mad."[91] Thus both Burton and Coeffeteau indicate as one cause of madness an experience parallel to that of Lysander, and the latter commentator specifically attributes the consequent violence to the temporary overthrow of the faculties of the rational soul. Exactly the same notion underlies Lemot's prophecy that by paying court to Florilla he will so heat Labervele's "jealous humour" that the old husband will run "start mad."[92]

Just as a hot, dry brain was understood to be giddy or

[89] *The Widow's Tears*, II, iii, 42–44.

[90] Burton defines such insanity as "a vehement *dotage*, or raving without a fever, far more violent than *melancholy*, full of anger and clamour, horrible looks, actions, gestures, troubling the patients with far greater vehemency both of body and mind, without all fear and sorrow, with such impetuous force & boldness, that sometimes three or four men cannot hold them. Differing only in this from *phrenzy*, that it is without a fever, and their memory is most part better. It hath the same causes as the other, as choler adust, and blood incensed, brains inflamed, etc."—*op. cit.*, I, 160–161.

[91] Coeffeteau, *op. cit.*, p. 23.

[92] *An Humourous Day's Mirth*, ii, 88–92.

even frenzied, so a cold, moist brain—the distemperature incited by conditions either constitutional or fleeting—was sottish and stupid.[93] The spirits were created to maintain instant communication between the faculties: memory in the rear of the brain, common sense or judgment in the center, and imagination in the front. It was supposed that the spirits could plod along only tardily if wet and chilled. Thus a page characterizes Captain Foulweather as "a dull moist-brained ass,"[94] and after spending a night in Lysander's tomb Ero exclaims: "So; let's air our dampish spirits, almost stifled in this gross muddy element."[95] Margaret, amused at Bassiolo's conscientious but uninspired effort to compose a love letter for her, explains his feeble wit in similar fashion:

> . . . I believe
> His muse lies in the back part of his brain,
> Which, thick and gross, is hard to be brought forward.[96]

In a similar passage, which is related also to ideas concerning both sleep and the absence of passion, Lodovico denies his unsuccessful attempt to force Lucretia. He declares that when he entered her chamber his thoughts were chaste, and that finding her asleep and desiring not to disturb her, he "lay down softly by her; when . . . in the very coldness and dulness of my spirit, I fell suddenly asleep."[97]

Upon occasion Chapman creates the impression that he is attempting to display his learning. Two such instances occur in his discussions of physiological processes. In the first, relatively unobstrusive passage the dramatist represents Monsieur D'Olive in the act of delivering an oration upon the merits of tobacco. The speaker insists that in his favorite plant

[93] Coeffeteau, *op. cit.*, Preface.   [94] *Sir Giles Goosecap*, I, i, 68.
[95] *The Widow's Tears*, IV, iii, 1–2.
[96] *The Gentleman Usher*, III, ii, 407–409.
[97] *May-Day*, V, i, 191–197.

are found all the elements composing the creation; for when the earthy tobacco is converted into fire, it gives off an airy vapor which, "ent'ring in at the mouth, walks through the regions of a man's brain, drives out all ill vapours but itself, draws down all bad humours by the mouth."[98]

In a much longer, dramatically indefensible dialogue the scholarly Clarence by the application of the Socratic method compels his physician, Doctor Versey, to retract his statement that Clarence is suffering from a "disease . . . rather of the mind than body." In brief the patient's argument is that physical "diseases" arise from "griefs" or disturbed states of feeling induced by passions, which in their turn "proceed from corporal distempers." There can be no analogous development of "disease" within the mind—by which term the scholar indirectly indicates that he means the rational soul—since passions and affections or feelings are found only in the sensible soul.[99] Nor can the ailments of the body influence the health of the mind; for to grant that the reasonable soul may interest itself voluntarily in the affairs of the sensitive soul, or that it may be compelled to take an interest in them, is to regard the rational soul as either a fool or a slave and so to attribute to it "far from that reason and freedom that the Empress of Reason and an eternal substance should comprehend." Clarence maintains that ignorance alone is a disease

---

[98] *Monsieur D'Olive*, II, ii, 252–258. Vicary, (*op. cit.*, pp. 39–44) refers frequently to discharges of the nose and throat as "superfluities of the brayne" which drop down to be expelled through the mouth. Although D'Olive's speech occurs in a farcical episode, yet he gives a fairly accurate description of what was supposed to take place when humours were driven from the brain.

[99] " . . . and *Affectus* your master Galen refers *parti irascenti*," Clarence reminds the doctor, "for *illic est anima sentiens ubi sunt affectus*; therefore the rational soul cannot be there also."—*Sir Giles Goosecap*, V, ii, 38–40.

of the mind, and by "ignorance" it may safely be assumed that he means failure to exercise the faculties of the rational soul. In answer to Versey's question Clarence denies that love is a disease of the mind, because "it springs naturally out of the blood" and is, consequently, a malady of the sensitive soul.[100]

Chapman, then, made extensive use of the physiological beliefs of the day, and of the psychology derived from them, in his attempt to portray and explain love, grief, anger, madness, stupidity—in a word all emotions and passions as well as certain mental traits. And while he may appear now and then to have been interested in impressing his audience with his scholarship, he was in general simply representative of his period. His constant purpose was not to baffle or to awe the spectators, but rather to assist them by explaining the nature and the experience of his creatures. In the employment of this device, as in the use of other expository methods, Chapman and the other Elizabethan dramatists were naïve. The playwright put direct explanations of character and of reaction into the speeches of persons who must expose their own inner nature, or into the remarks of others whom he selected to perform that revelation for them.

[100] *Sir Giles Goosecap*, V, ii, 1–51.

CHAPTER VIII

CHAPMAN AND THE COMEDY OF HUMOURS

THE frequent references to humours in the preceding chapter indicate that those fluids were believed to exert a considerable influence in the determination of character. Although the conception of human nature which underlies the comedy of humours was no more an accurate reflection of contemporary scientific thought than literary and popular notions usually are, the materials of such drama were presented and accepted as psychological. There can be no doubt that there was a definite connection between the lore and the art of the day.[1]

The terms "humour" and "humourous," which con-

---

[1] Humour psychology, the personification of abstractions (in the morality plays and elsewhere), the example of eccentric but wholly conventional characters in Latin and Italian comedy, the idea of decorum (which welded specified traits to character types), and the interest in books of "Characters" (English examples of which, however, did not appear in final form until the early years of the sevententh century), all contributed to the development of the comedy of humours. Professor Charles Read Baskervill presents an excellent exposition of this subject in his *English Elements in Jonson's Early Comedy*, pp. 39–75. Among other discussions of the subject may be mentioned Charles Mills Gayley's *Plays of Our Forefathers*, pp. 297–298, 314, and his *Representative English Comedies*, II, xx; Charles H. Herford and Percy Simpson's *Ben Jonson*, I, 338–341; Professor Simpson's edition of *Every Man in His Humour*, pp. xxxvii–xxxviii; Mina Kerr's *The Influence of Ben Jonson on English Comedy, 1598–1642*, pp. 12–13; Elizabeth Woodbridge's *Studies in Jonson's Comedy*, pp. 24–37; Felix E. Schelling's *Elizabethan Drama*, I, 454–471, his *English Literature during the Lifetime of Shakespeare*, pp. 230–232, and his *Foreign Influences in Elizabethan Plays*, pp. 19–26; and Joel Elias Springarn's *A History of Literary Criticism in the Renaissance*, pp. 87–88.

stantly reappear in Elizabethan titles and dialogue, had undergone a fairly rapid expansion of meaning.[2] It is obvious,
for example, that something beyond the narrowly medical
significance must be understood if such a creature as Morose
is to be accepted as a study in humours. It is difficult to understand how any comedy, and least of all such satirical comedy
as Jonson and Chapman wrote, could be successful or even
justifiable if the central figure were regarded as a mere problem in pathology. A grotesque figure like Morose becomes
ludicrous when he is so extravagantly distorted that he assumes the impersonal nature of the manikin associated with
farce. When his peculiarity is of the self-centered type always
found in drama of humours, his futile, meaningless activity
mocks the feverish but narrow spirit of the superman of the
sixteenth-century stage and his ranting burlesques the heroics
of bombastic Elizabethan drama.[3]

By the time Chapman and Jonson developed their
unique comedy the word "humour" had come to refer to
irregular conduct prompted less by physiological disturbances than by distorted social conceptions perpetuated and
aggravated by unbelievable stupidity. Those who suffer in
this drama are almost invariably the obtuse rather than the
immoral.[4] In the old physiological sense jealousy, affectation, and infatuated vanity would be much less "humourous"
than cruelty and lust; yet in Chapman and Jonson the former qualities are regarded as more culpable than the latter.[5]

[2] Baskervill, op. cit., pp. 39–75; but cf. Simpson, op. cit., p. xxxvii,
note 1.

[3] For a related point of view see Herford and Simpson, op. cit.,
I, 340–341.

[4] This fact, which contradicts Jonson's protestation of a moral pur-
pose in his comedies, has often been pointed out by students of his plays.
See, for example, Woodbridge, op. cit., pp. 29–31, and Maurice Castelain,
Ben Jonson; l'homme et l'œuvre, pp. 512–513.

[5] Cf. Herford and Simpson, op. cit., I, 341.

Thus humourous traits lose their grim inevitability and be-come simply comic foibles.[6]

Comedy of humours is distinguished in part by its epi-sodic structure. Around the singular character or characters the dramatist groups a number of either related or disjoined incidents, the purpose of which seems to be not the advance-ment of a continuous narrative but the examination of pecu-liarities under varied circumstances.[7] Those of Jonson's and Chapman's plays which most insistently depict the victims of the weird social and moral obsessions which humours had come to be are little more than galleries filled with row upon row of portraits of leering idiots.

It may be true that Chapman was an experimenter who did not develop any finished products illustrative of the genre;[8] but the humour motif is clearly evident in the entire range of his comedies. His earliest extant dramatic composi-tion, *The Blind Beggar of Alexandria*, is described on the title-page of 1598 as "most pleasantly discoursing his variable humours in disguised shapes full of conceite and pleasure."[9] Italianate intrigue so dominates the plot that personages cannot merely display their eccentricities through a succes-sion of relatively disconnected antics, but the words "hu-mour" and "humourous" are conspicuous in the dialogue, and Cleanthes has as many humours as disguises. Similarly, despite the fact that in his last comedy, *The Widow's Tears*, Chapman presents Lysander's jealousy seriously, it is indis-

[6] Gayley, *Representative English Comedies*, II, xxvi.

[7] This characteristic of the comedy of humours is emphasized by, for example, Baskervill, *op. cit.*, p. 107; Woodbridge, *op. cit.*, pp. 24, 48, 57; Kerr, *op. cit.*, pp. 11, 14; Herford and Simpson, *op. cit.*, I, 343; and Castelain, *op. cit.*, pp. 218–220, 250.

[8] Such an assertion is made by Herford and Simpson, *op. cit.*, I, 345, and by Tucker Brooke, *The Tudor Drama*, pp. 405–406.

[9] See Parrott, *The Comedies of George Chapman*, p. 673.

putable that his hero is a humourous type whose foible demands correction. One may contend that characterization and
situation dependent on humours are present in practically all
of Chapman's comic plays; at the same time one must concede that such characters, incidents, and bits of conversation
are presented solely for their independent value in only a
few of his works.

If Henslowe's "comodey of vmers" of May 11, 1597,[10]
be, as many judge,[11] Chapman's *An Humourous Day's
Mirth*, this dramatist actually preceded Jonson in putting a
bona fide comedy of humours upon the stage. However the
question of priority may be decided, it is certain that all the
technique of the new fashion is displayed in the play just
named. All persons characterized even to a slight degree,
though they be only the old stock figures, are dominated
by humours. Moreover the playwright devotes entire scenes
to character exposition, neglecting to advance his story while
his queer and unimportant creatures parade their follies *ad
libitum*.

In this comedy Blanuel and Dowsecer are genuine creatures of humours. Neither is of the least importance in the
tenuous plot, if plot *An Humourous Day's Mirth* can be said
to have, and neither spends much time upon the stage. Both
men are elaborately characterized as studies in humours before they appear, and neither one does anything except to
display his peculiarity.

Before Blanuel makes his initial entry, Lemot, who acts

[10] *Henslowe's Diary*, edited by W. W. Greg, I, 52, line 27.

[11] See, for example, Herford and Simpson, *op. cit.*, I, 343; Greg, *op.
cit.*, II, 184; Parrott, *op. cit.*, p. 685; Kerr, *op. cit.*, pp. 20–21; Baskervill,
op. cit., p. 37; Schelling, *Elizabethan Drama*, I, 460; etc. Presenting a
different conclusion, Gayley, *Representative English Comedies*, I, 526–528,
533, proposes, as a substitute for Chapman's play, Henry Porter's *The Two
Angry Women of Abington*.

as ringmaster throughout the performance of the entire
menagerie, describes him as a clumsy creature who will perform his repertoire of two mechanical social tricks. He will
repeat verbatim whatever conventional compliments may be
addressed to him, and then, the amenities exhausted, he will
adopt a pose of profound, speechless, cross-armed melancholy.[12] Lemot's preparatory exposition concludes with the
announcement, "See where he comes"; and Blanuel stalks
out to exhibit, with perfect fidelity to every detail, the accomplishments which have already been attributed to him. At the
time of entering and of leaving he is, as Lemot says, "your
complete ape," and during the interim he leans against the
chimney corner, a witless image of melancholy.[13] In his few
brief subsequent appearances Blanuel is no longer the pic-
turesque individual; he is a typical, thoroughly unobtrusive
gallant.[14]

Dowsecer is as inconsequential as Blanuel. In a preliminary characterization Dowsecer is discussed as overcome with
scholarly melancholy—some say lunacy—and so detached
from the allurements of physical life that his old father,
Count Labervele, sadly foresees the extinction of his house.[15]
After a long scene in which his rather impressive misanthropy

[12] *An Humourous Day's Mirth*, ii, 24–51.

[13] *Ibid.*, ii, 52–109. There is a similar and equally purposeless scene
later (viii, 206–251) in which Lemot successfully forecasts the speeches
of Rowley, Labesha, Foyes, Berger, and Moren. This later scene, however, appears to be as much a satire on the stale wits of the day as it is
a study of humours.

[14] In Scene v Blanuel speaks four unimportant lines which have no
relation to his eccentricity or to the plot; his appearance in Scene viii is
equally pointless. Stage directions for Scene xii mention him as entering,
but he takes no part in either the action or the dialogue of that Scene.
He may be supposed to be included in the miscellaneous groups in Scenes
vii, xiii, and xiv, but he is not named specifically and he has no lines.

[15] *An Humourous Day's Mirth*, vii, 15–64.

is grossly dragged out and exhibited for the entertainment of the curious King and his frivolous companions,[16] Dowsecer withdraws into a seclusion from which he does not return until the close of the play. Still scholarly though no longer melancholy, he revisits the earth barely in time to be betrothed to Martia. His love affair is dramatically quite unsatisfactory in itself and has no plot meaning or connection.

Chapman seems to have taken this congenial personage somewhat seriously. The King, even before he has seen Dowsecer, informs his comrades that, while idle gossip has it that the young man is afflicted with lunacy,[17] the better opinion is that he suffers from a sadness induced by overmuch study.[18] Thus does the satiric scholar-dramatist establish the fact that Dowsecer's misanthropic cynicism proceeds from a wisdom exceeding that of other men.[19] As Dowsecer, unaware of his eavesdropping audience, proceeds with his self-revelation, both the reckless King and the giddy Martia are sobered by the conviction that they are observing the operation of a mind which is not shattered by insanity but inspired by extraordinary understanding.[20]

---

[16] *Ibid.*, vii, 65–216.

[17] For the contemporary scientific explanation of moon madness see Vicary, *The Anatomie of the Bodie of Man*, pp. 33–34.

[18] Burton (*The Anatomy of Melancholy*, I, 348–350) tells why *"students dote more often than others."* His assertion that too much attention to books weakens the body, dulls the spirits, and destroys courage is wholly applicable to Dowsecer, as is also his explanation of the absence of natural passions. It is in an effort to arouse these dormant interests that Lavel places garments, a sword, and the portrait of the beautiful Martia where Dowsecer cannot fail to find them (see *An Humourous Day's Mirth*, vii, 51–64).

[19] *An Humourous Day's Mirth*, vii, 15–22.

[20] *Ibid.*, vii, 87–90, 136–137, 196–197. On this pleasure trip to Labervele's private Bedlam, Martia falls in love with the inmate whose antics she has come to observe.

Dowsecer's activity in this, his only scene of any duration or interest, is threefold: he soliloquizes at length in the approved scholarly and melancholy manner;[21] he expresses his unbounded, absolute disgust with life, marriage, and the reproduction of the race;[22] and he gives certain indications of his incipient love for Martia.[23] The first and second actions are strictly in accord with the rôle of the melancholy hero. Musings and railings against life, and especially against the sex proclivities of the human race, are typical of such stage figures.[24] His hint of awakening love is a prophecy of the way in which he is to be put out of his humour; for, as he explains later, the heat of the passion of love is so much greater than that of the vanity of melancholy that admiration for the lady quite takes possession of his faculties.[25]

Under the influence of this new experience, Dowsecer escapes from his morbidity and becomes a surprisingly dashing gallant. When he appears upon the stage for the last time, he thunders out threats in a fashion well nigh irreconcilable with his earlier detached and disinterested superiority. Discovering an attraction in his social environment, he has cast aside his scholarly reticence and melancholy and has recov-

[21] Lines 65–156 of Scene vii of *An Humourous Day's Mirth* are solid soliloquy, interrupted only by the explanatory and directive comments of the spying King and his fellows.

[22] *Ibid.*, vii, 164–189.

[23] *Ibid.*, vii, 199–216.

[24] Note, for example, Hamlet's frequent soliloquies and his recurrent condemnations of lasciviousness. Dowsecer's vituperations have no such immediate provocation as have Hamlet's, for although his stepmother, Florilla, is no better than she should be, Dowsecer seems ignorant of her existence. Shakespeare's Jaques, Marston's Malevole, and Jonson's Macilente display similar inclinations. For detailed discussion see E. E. Stoll's "Shaksper, Marston, and the Malcontent Type," *MP*, III (1906), 281–303.

[25] *An Humourous Day's Mirth*, xiv, 94–96.

ered the vigor and the martial spirit, as well as the consciousness of his own body, of which studiousness has heretofore
deprived him. Madly jealous of the King's attentions to
Martia, he vows:

> I'll geld the adulterous goat, and take from him
> The instrument that plays him such sweet music.[26]

The King has spoken wisely: "the sense doth still stir up the
soul."[27]

In addition to the two purely humourous characters,
Blanuel and Dowsecer, there are in this comedy many stock
figures which Chapman presents through the technique of the
comedy of humours.[28] These are the usual jealous husbands
and wives, the foolish lovers, the ridiculous fathers, and the
other puppets who hold the relationships always found in
stereotyped intrigue comedy, and hence are much more inte-
gral parts of the comedy than are Blanuel and Dowsecer. At
the same time, like all humourous characters, they do nothing
and arrive nowhere.

These stage personages are aimless largely because Chapman has failed to give them much to do. There is a slight,
barely traceable plot, but there are numerous scenes which
have not even the most indirect connection with it.[29] Some of

---

[26] *Ibid.*, xiv, 52–53. Psychologically, the heat of passion has trans-
formed his cold, dry (melancholy) humour to a hot, dry (choleric) one.

[27] *Ibid.*, vii, 61.

[28] Such characters are Labervele, Florilla, Labesha, Foyes, and the
Countess Moren, all of whom have already been discussed in some detail as type figures. Herford and Simpson (*op. cit.*, I, 344) regard
Labervele and Countess Moren as the most satisfactorily "humourous"
creatures in this play.

[29] Scenes v, vii, viii, xi, and xii of *An Humourous Day's Mirth* are
mere character sketches or cartoons. Castelain's criticism of Jonson's plots
(*Ben Jonson; l'homme et l'œuvre*, p. 244) is equally applicable to Chapman's.

the episodes which do assist the feeble story are interrupted by prolonged passages inserted only to depict eccentricities.[30] Practically every scene which is of any appreciable length is developed either wholly or principally to serve this subsidiary purpose.

An Humourous Day's Mirth, then, approaches the comedy of humours in that it contains two elaborately and carefully portrayed humorous characters, Blanuel and Dowsecer; employs the caricaturist's method to reveal certain stock comic figures; and devotes practically all its effort to the exposition of grotesque personages, and so allows the tenuous plot to lapse completely in scene after scene in order to make way for action which is futile except as an exposure of folly.

Cornelio, the jealous husband of Gazetta in *All Fools*, is largely a humourous type.[31] In a detailed exposition preparatory to his first appearance his wife describes him as one "vainly jealous," so unreasonable that he is suspicious of her every move and yet so crafty that he does his best to conceal his anxiety lest he teach her to betray him.[32] As she concludes her remarks, he blusters onto the stage and, with the illuminating explanation that he believes women always are plotting mischief, orders Gazetta into the house. As she turns to leave she observes to her companions: "These humours reign in marriage; humours, humours!"[33]

---

[30] In Scenes iv and xiii plot and humour revelation are of practically equal importance, and in Scenes vi and ix intrusions are evident.

[31] Cornelio is represented, too, as something of a bumpkin, though Chapman does not develop that side of his character. In *All Fools*, I, ii, 37, Gazetta refers to Cornelio's former "farmer's state"; and in II, i, 241–242, he speaks of himself as a peasant. One is reminded that in the Restoration comedy of manners the gay young wife of the countryman was legitimate game for any adventurous city gentleman.

[32] *All Fools*, I, ii, 20–35.

[33] *Ibid.*, I, ii, 52–53. Gratiana, a companion, remarks (lines 56–57) that " 't were indecorum This heifer [Cornelio] should want horns." The

When Cornelio discovers Gazetta sewing upon a flower-bedecked piece, he is so convinced of her intention to send it to her lover as a semiconcealed amorous confession that he bluntly accuses her of an affair with Dariotto.[34] As the angered wife leaves the stage Cornelio explains to the audience that since he prefers to be known as a "jealous ass, and not a wittolly knave," his treatment of Gazetta is merely protective. He declares that he has no intention of relaxing his vigilance.[35]

With Cornelio jealousy is a mania. He takes a morbid satisfaction in considering himself a cuckold. No one can convince him of his error, and the prospect of discovering that his wife is innocent has not the slightest attraction for him. As Valerio asks, "Who can assure a jealous spirit?"[36] Throughout the play he is spoken of as mad with jealousy.[37] He is long and frequently upon the stage, and practically all his time is devoted to a display of his humour.[38]

Eventually this miserable creature is literally talked out of his humour. Although most of the personages fall readily into the conventional readjustments of the closing scenes of the play, Cornelio remains unsatisfied, obstinately insistent upon divorcing Gazetta. After the young gallants have failed to make any impression upon him, the old fathers, Marc. Antonio and Gostanzo, undertake to dissuade him. By re-

---

bovine metaphor seems to have appealed to Chapman as appropriate to the rustic; for again in III, i, 310, Dariotto asks, "Why, is the bull run mad?" In Gratiana's speech the reference to decorum perhaps is not to be taken very seriously; yet Chapman probably used the expression deliberately, with the intention of suggesting that, according to the principle invoked, horns invariably accompany the jealous humour.

[34] *Ibid.*, II, i, 232–270.   [36] *Ibid.*, III, i, 142–158.
[35] *Ibid.*, II, i, 272–295.   [37] *Ibid.*, III, i, 300, 310; V, i, 17–23; etc.
[38] The exceptions occur in *All Fools*, II, i, 367–428, where Cornelio gulls Valerio, and in V, 1, 24–75, where he plots revenge for the trick which Valerio and his cronies have put upon him.

minding him of how much his father wisely endured from his mate—for Cornelio's mother, too, had her humour, says Gostanzo—they finally elicit from him the declaration that never has he intended to treat his wife more harshly than was necessary "to bridle her stout stomach."[39]

Out of this confused story of much talk and little action, this story "full of sound and fury, signifying nothing," the humourous character of Cornelio emerges. How little Chapman cared about the plot is evident from the fact that from start to finish the position of Gazetta is ambiguous. Cornelio's jealous humour can rage equally well whether she be true or disloyal to him.

In *Sir Giles Goosecap* there are three humourous characters, all distinguished by peculiarities of speech and by mere surface mannerisms of conduct rather than by fundamental, psychological idiosyncrasies. As Blanuel assumes a melancholy which he does not feel and as Cornelio wilfully maintains a jealous exterior for reasons of policy, these men create the impression of unintelligent artificiality. All are minutely described before they set foot upon the stage.[40]

Sir Giles is an effeminate, apish simpleton whose distinctive weaknesses, his inability to understand the mother tongue and his persistent self-contradiction, have already received detailed consideration.[41] Captain Foulweather, something of a hero in this fantastic coterie because he has visited the continent, belittles Englishmen and their manners and affects

[39] *All Fools*, V, ii, 158–230. Cornelio's statement is consistent with his early explanation of his conduct as merely precautionary; but his violent attack upon Dariotto (III, i, 335–360) indicates the degree to which his frenzied humour dominates his action.

[40] *Sir Giles Goosecap*, I, i, 47–130.

[41] In Chapter VI, where he is discussed as a typical lout. For a statement of his lady-like accomplishments see especially *Sir Giles Goosecap*, II, i, 285–334.

French taste and interests. He has an individual way of piling up adjectives, nouns, phrases, and other elements of expression. This practice is similar to but not identical with the pedant's habit. His favorite word, which he delights in using or misusing regardless of context, is "emphatical."[42] Sir Cuthbert Rudesby is blunt and sullen and his comments are invariably gruff. He seems intent on giving offense, but strangely enough no one is provoked to resent his boorishness. He may insult his hostess, Lady Eugenia,[43] and he may heap abuse upon the conceited head of Captain Foulweather;[44] but among these marionettes nothing matters because nothing is real.

In this comedy, as in *An Humourous Day's Mirth* and *All Fools*, Chapman writes many scenes which possess no dramatic significance but which clearly reveal the foibles of his farcical personages.[45] *Sir Giles Goosecap* boasts no secondary plot; the episodes in which the whimsical triumvirate functions are so disconnected that they tell no story; they are simply incidents revealing character. Detached as these creatures are from the principal action, the mildly appealing love story of Eugenia and Clarence, they completely overshadow it. The progress of the main plot often is retarded while Chapman presents and repeats the exposition of Sir Giles, Foulweather, and Rudesby.

[42] *Sir Giles Goosecap*, I, ii, 10–13, 53–55, 67–74, 77–80. Goosecap likewise has a favorite phrase: "Because we are all mortal." See I, i, 110–112; I, ii, 35; etc.

[43] *Ibid.*, I, ii, 1–2, 28–29.   [44] *Ibid.*, I, ii, 53–66.

[45] *Ibid.*, I, i, ii, iii; III, i; IV, ii; most of V, i, and the first and last parts of V, ii, are devoted practically entirely to the antics of these three men; parts of II, i, and IV, i, add to the picturization of their humours; but the first and most thorough revelation of them is given in I, ii.

APPENDIXES

APPENDIX A
NOTES ON THE LIFE AND WRITINGS OF CHAPMAN

ASIDE from details connected with the publication of his works little is definitely known about the life of George Chapman. Unhampered by the·presence of facts by which to check their theories, writers have hazarded various suppositions concerning his private affairs. Swinburne cautiously guessed that the dramatist may have seen military service in the Netherlands under Sir Francis Vere.[1] As Swinburne realized, the evidence is flimsy. It consists of two facts, that Chapman is lost from sight from 1576 or 1578, when he left the university, until 1594, when he published his first poem, *The Shadow of Night*, and that in this work there is a long, elaborate account of a complicated military maneuver executed at one point in Vere's campaign.[2]

It was Swinburne, too, who first suggested that Chapman's cynical comedy, *The Widow's Tears*, was prompted by a widow's refusal to marry him.[3] This alluring speculation receives substantial support from a group of letters recently discovered and made public.[4] It is clear that the author of these missives carried on negotiations with a widow; that

[1] Algernon Charles Swinburne, "Essay on George Chapman's Poetical and Dramatic Works," p. xxii, in Swinburne's edition of *The Works of George Chapman: Poems and Minor Translations* (1875).

[2] The prolonged simile which induced Swinburne to make this statement occurs on page 14 of Swinburne's *The Works of George Chapman*.

[3] Swinburne, *op. cit.*, p. xxxi.

[4] These letters, in part printed and in part summarized by Bertram Dobell in the *Athenaeum* from March 23 to April 13, 1901, are not

after meeting and falling in love at the home of a common friend, the widow and her suitor disagreed, evidently over the terms of the marriage settlement; and that the gentleman left in a fit of bad temper. Then in a letter to his host he apologizes for his brusqueness, attributing it to a "bashfull and uncourtly simplicitie" which caused him to withdraw from a place where he might not be wholly welcome. He requests his friend to copy and to send to the widow as his own an enclosed letter, the most interesting part of which informs her that a brother has agreed to supply the disappointed suitor with means to complete the settlement to the lady's satisfaction. The host is urged to advise her that she will do well to accept so worthy a lover. Other letters, which appear to have been dispatched from the writer directly to his lady, vary in tone from ardent courtship, adoration mingled with extravagant protestations of everlasting humility and service, to vile and bitter denunciation, and seem to indicate that the relation between the parties terminated in a permanent breach.

Scholars differ in their attitudes toward the widow hypothesis.[5] Ignoring the questions which probably always will remain, one can adduce a little negative evidence. None of the biographical references to Chapman state that he was married. Some letters almost certainly written by Chapman are related to his imprisonment for offenses in *Eastward Ho!*,

---

originals, but copies lacking date, superscription, and signature. Mr. Dobell, however, was convinced that some of them were written by Chapman. On this point see his comment in the *Athenaeum*, March 23, 1901, p. 369.

[5] Mr. Dobell (*Athenaeum*, March 23, 1901, p. 369) thinks it "most probable that Chapman was unsuccessful in his wooing of the widow" and "likely that his comedy of 'The Widow's Tears' . . . was inspired by his own experiences with the lady to whom the above letter was addressed." Professor Schoell accepts the theory (cf. Parrott, *The Comedies of George Chapman*, p. 803); but Professor Parrott (*ibid.*) rejects the notion as illogical.

to the persecution to which he was subjected at the instigation of the French ambassador because of objectionable material in *The Conspiracy and Tragedy of Byron*, to the appalling poverty into which he was cast by the sudden death of his patron, Prince Henry, and to danger of persecution and imprisonment for debt. Yet not one of these letters mentions anyone except the writer as suffering or likely to suffer. There is no reference to a wife or a child.

Other speculative attempts to supplement the few ascertained biographical facts have resulted in the construction of elaborate arguments to prove that Chapman is the Rival Poet of Shakespeare's *Sonnets*[6] and that he is the original of whom Holofernes in *Love's Labour's Lost* is a burlesque.[7]

Unfortunately no contemporary biographer left a mass of authentic data concerning the dramatist's life. His birthplace is supposed to be Hitchin;[8] and although there is contemporary documentary support for two different birthdates,[9] it is now believed that Chapman was born in 1559. Chapman, who is generally understood to have been a university man, gained a reputation as the translator of Homer's poems, and he inserted a number of classical references into his original poems and into his plays, even his comedies. Yet his actual knowledge of Greek and Latin was challenged by scholars of

[6] Arthur Acheson, *Shakespeare and the Rival Poet*; J. M. Robertson, *Shakespeare and Chapman* · and *The Problems of the Shakespeare Sonnets.*

[7] Robertson, *Shakespeare and Chapman*, pp. 110–116.

[8] See the "Inductio" to *The Tears of Peace*, p. 112 of Swinburne's 1875 edition of Chapman's poems, and William Browne's *Britannia's Pastorals*, Book II, Song II, 281–283.

[9] Anthony à Wood, *Athenae Oxonienses*, II, 262, says that Chapman was seventy-two years old when he died in 1634, but there is little reason to doubt the accuracy of the inscription under the portrait at the beginning of *The Whole Works of Homer, Prince of Poets*: "Georgius Chapmannus, Homeri Metaphrastes. Aeta LVII. MDCXVI."

his own time,[10] and recent critics have questioned especially his familiarity with the Greek language.[11]

Of one fact there is ample evidence, Chapman's impecuniosity. *Henslowe's Diary* catalogues loan after loan made to Chapman in sums ranging from ten shillings to three pounds.[12] Although these aids are recorded as advance payments on work which the dramatist was doing for Henslowe, they indicate that Chapman earned his living with his pen and that often he found it necessary to spend his money before he had quite earned it. Further indication of the same fact is revealed in some of the letters recently discovered, which represent the dramatist as in bad financial circumstances.[13] An older man now, he urges his former usefulness as an argument for pecuniary assistance. He begs to be spared further epistolary persecution for debt. At first frigidly dignified because insulted, he soon assures his creditor that he will pay as soon as he can. He ends in a conciliatory key, informing his tormenter that he has often owed larger sums for longer periods. Another letter describes his destitution following the

[10] In his "Preface to the Reader" accompanying *Homer's Iliads* the poet admits that he has been accused by incompetent and envious spirits of translating Homer from the French instead of the Greek. Indignantly he denies the accusation. See *The Works of George Chapman: Homer's Iliad and Odyssey* (R. H. Shepherd, 1875), pp. 4–5.

[11] Professors Legouis and Schoell believe that Chapman had little acquaintance with the original Greek writings. See Schoell's *Études sur l'humanisme continental en Angleterre à la fin de la Renaissance, passim,* but especially pp. vi and 6.

[12] See W. W. Greg's edition of *Henslowe's Diary,* for instance the following passages of Vol. I: p. 86, lines 26–28; p. 87, lines 10–12; p. 88, lines 1–3; p. 110, lines 9–12. On page 142, lines 1–8, occurs an acknowledgment of indebtedness over Chapman's signature; the amount is £10 10*s.*

[13] Bertram Dobell's articles, as listed, under dates March 23 and April 6. Some of the papers bear Chapman's signature; Mr. Dobell believes he wrote them all.

death of Henry, Prince of Wales. Encouraged by his royal patron, Chapman had agreed to continue his translation of Homer, with the result that when Henry died the poet was burdened with serious responsibilities which he had incurred in the course of the undertaking and of which he had expected the Prince to relieve him. Still another evidence of Chapman's indigence is found in a poem by John Davies of Hereford, in which the writer attempts to reconcile his fellow-poet to his poverty by reminding him that art is always poorly rewarded and by suggesting that what Chapman lacks of this world's goods is more than compensated for by the "Treasures of arte" which he has in his "head and hart and hand."[14] Since Davies confesses that he knows Chapman only by his works, these commendatory verses suggest that the playwright's financial troubles may have been widely known, while the fact that the evidences here given cover a long span of years indicates that the condition was recurrent if not chronic.[15]

The earliest reference to any of Chapman's dramatic works is Henslowe's entry of £3 received at the performance of "the blind beger of elexandrea" on February 12, 1595/6.[16] The popularity of this coarse, crudely constructed, extravagant play is an incontrovertible proof of the debased popular taste in the early days of Chapman and Shakespeare.[17] Even

[14] *John Davies of Hereford,* edited for the Chertsey Worthies' Library by Alexander B. Grosart. The poem, one of the brief compositions "To Worthy Persons," is entitled "To my highly vallued Mr George Chapman, Father of our English Poets," and is printed in *The Scourge of Folly,* II, 59–60.

[15] Henslowe's payments to Chapman, nearly a dozen, were made during 1598 and 1599; Grosart believes that the poem by Davies was published in 1611; Prince Henry died in 1612. Chapman's name disappears from Henslowe's records during 1599 and does not reappear.

[16] Greg's *Henslowe's Diary,* I, 28, line 22.

[17] Charles J. Sisson's *Le Goût public et le théâtre elisabéthain jusqu'à*

after making generous allowance for the fact that this first work has been preserved in an incomplete manuscript, it is impossible to imagine that the now mutilated romantic plot could ever have softened the glaring comic action to any appreciable degree. Yet Henslowe offered the play twenty-two times during the fourteen months following the entry, generally with good gate receipts.[18] Moreover the records in the *Diary* show that late in the spring of 1601 the industrious producer was advancing money for a revival of the old comedy.[19]

Apparently Chapman had won his public. Such was his reputation in 1598 that Francis Meres was willing to name him in *Palladis Tamia* as one of the best English writers of both comedy and tragedy.[20] By what plays this fame had been established it is impossible to determine, for it is believed that Chapman's earliest extant tragedy, *Bussy D'Ambois*, was not written before 1603,[21] and the only surviving and identified comedies in existence as early as 1598 were *The Blind Beggar of Alexandria* and *An Humourous Day's Mirth*.[22]

From Meres's acceptance of Chapman's position as established and from other statements it appears that not all the playwright's work is extant, or else that not all of it has been identified. Henslowe, for example, made payments to Chap-

---

la morte de Shakespeare is an interesting analysis of the artistic ideals of the London playgoing bourgeoisie.

[18] See Greg's edition of the *Diary*, I, 28–51.

[19] *Ibid.*, I, 136–138.

[20] G. Gregory Smith, *Elizabethan Critical Essays*, II, 319–320, where extracts from *Palladis Tamia* are reprinted.

[21] Parrott (*The Tragedies of George Chapman*, p. 541) thinks the play was not written before the death of Elizabeth. Other scholars (e.g. Chambers, *The Elizabethan Stage*, III, 253) agree in assigning a late date to the play.

[22] Assuming that Henslowe's "comodey of vmers" (*Henslowe's Diary*, I, 52, line 27) was Chapman's *An Humourous Day's Mirth*.

man on a "pastrall tragedie" and *The Iyll of a Womon*;[23]
but neither of these plays is known. Nor does *The Fount of
New Fashions*, completed in the autumn of 1598,[24] exist
unless Fleay's temerarious conjecture be correct, that *The
Isle of Women*,[25] *The Fount of New Fashions*, and *Monsieur
D'Olive* all are names for the same play.[26] Warburton's cook,
too, is supposed to have destroyed two of Chapman's plays,
The Yorkshire Gentlewoman and Her Son and *Fatal Love,
a French Tragedy*.[27]

Further proof of Chapman's popularity as a dramatist is
afforded by the posthumous publication of works unjustifiably
ascribed to him. In 1654, twenty years after his death, he was
named as author upon the title-page of two tragedies, *Revenge for Honour* and *The Tragedy of Alphonsus, Emperor
of Germany*, although he probably did not write them.[28]
Almost equally erroneous, or deliberately misleading, was
the publication in 1639 of *The Ball* as a comedy composed
jointly by Chapman and James Shirley; for it is generally
agreed that at most Chapman's part in the construction was
limited to the revision of a few lines.[29]

[23] Entries in the *Diary* for July 17, 1599 (I, 110, lines 9–12), and
June 15, 1598 (I, 88, lines 1–3), respectively.
[24] Greg's *Henslowe's Diary*, I, 96, lines 7–9; 97, lines 4–6.
[25] Also called *The Will of a Woman*; see Parrott, *The Comedies of
George Chapman*, p. 775, note 1.
[26] F. G. Fleay, *A Biographical Chronicle of the English Drama*, I, 59.
[27] See *The Dictionary of National Biography*, X, 51–52; *The Cambridge History of English Literature*, VI, 40; and Fleay, *op. cit.*, I, 66.
When these plays were entered with the Stationers on June 29, 1660,
they were listed as written by Chapman. See *A Transcript of the Registers of the Worshipful Company of Stationers, 1640–1708* (privately
printed in London, 1915), II, 271.
[28] Professor Parrott summarizes the evidence on both sides of the
question in *The Tragedies of George Chapman*, considering the authorship of *Alphonsus, Emperor of Germany* on pages 683–686, and the authorship of *Revenge for Honour* on pages 713–717.
[29] See Parrott, *The Comedies of George Chapman*, p. 872; *The Dic-*

Chapman's literary activity was varied and prolonged. Composing comedies, so far as present scholarship knows, from 1595 to 1605, he penned tragedies from 1603 to 1613.[30] His first publication of nondramatic poetry occurred in 1594; in 1598 he completed Marlowe's *Hero and Leander* and released the first two volumes of translations from Homer, a work carried forward by the publication in 1616 of his rendition of the two Homeric epics and completed by the appearance in 1624 of a volume in which he gathered up what he had not previously translated. Meanwhile he was issuing his original verse. His productive period covers at least the years 1594 to 1624.

Chapman died May 12, 1634.

---

tionary of National Biography, X, 51; *The Cambridge History of English Literature,* VI, 227; Robert S. Forsythe, *The Relations of Shirley's Plays to the Elizabethan Drama,* pp. 9, 407–409; Arthur H. Nason, *James Shirley, Dramatist,* p. 100; Chambers, *The Elizabethan Stage,* III, 260.

[30] The dates are based upon Professor Parrott's studies of Chapman's comedies and tragedies. Not all other scholars agree with his conclusions.

APPENDIX B

THE DATES OF CHAPMAN'S COMEDIES

THE following table, intended primarily for quick reference, shows that among outstanding students of Elizabethan drama there is fair uniformity of opinion concerning the years in which Chapman composed his various comedies, and that it is generally supposed that he was through with comedy by 1605 or 1606; Sir Edmund K. Chambers alone, of the scholars listed here, favors a later date. The plays are arranged chronologically, with Professor Parrott's judgment as guide.

Play	Parrott[1]	Schelling[2]	Chambers[3]	Gayley[4]
		Dates assigned by		
The Blind Beggar of Alexandria	1595–96	1595–96	1596	1596
An Humourous Day's Mirth	1597	1597	1597	1597
All Fools	1599	1599	1604?	1602 or 3
May-Day	1601 or 2	1601	c. 1609	1600 or 1
The Gentleman Usher	1602	1602?	1602?	1601 or 2
Sir Giles Goosecap	1601 to 3	1601	1601 to 3	1601
Monsieur D'Olive	1605	1605	1604	1604
Eastward Ho!	1605	1605	1605	1604 or 5
The Widow's Tears	1605 or 6	1605	1603 to 9	1602

[1] Parrott, *The Comedies of George Chapman*, introductions to the separate plays.

[2] Schelling, *Elizabethan Drama*, I, 460–463.

[3] Chambers, *The Elizabethan Stage*, III, 251–256; IV, 15–16.

[4] Gayley, *Representative English Comedies*, II, lii.

NOTE—Professor Elmer Edgar Stoll, in his article "On the Date of Some of Chapman's Plays," MP, XX (1905), 206–209, states only that, of the comedies, *Monsieur D'Olive* and *The Widow's Tears* must have been composed at some time "previous to 1605."

APPENDIX C

THE IDENTIFICATION AND EXPOSITION OF CHARACTERS IN COMEDIES OF ELIZABETHAN DRAMATISTS OTHER THAN CHAPMAN, WITH NOTES ON EPITHETIC CHARACTERIZATION AND DISGUISED FIGURES

THIS Appendix supplies, from Elizabethan comedies other than those of Chapman, a list of references sufficiently widespread to show that the practices of character identification and exposition examined in the second and third chapters were actually conventional.

The accompanying table contains titles of plays both earlier than Chapman's first comedy and later than his final one in order to demonstrate that the conventions existed, often in a cruder and less hidden form, before Chapman began to write and persisted after he ceased; in other words, to remove any possible suspicion that those practical expedients to which Chapman resorted were in his day either novel or outworn. The comedies of John Lyly are the earliest ones considered, and the latest were composed from five to ten years after Chapman had turned from comedy to tragedy. In order further to demonstrate the universality of the practices tabulated here, there have been entered under each heading at least two references to Shakespearean comedies.

Choice was limited voluntarily to the better-known and more respected dramatists writing comedy between approximately 1585 and 1610, and an effort was made to catalogue only plays which are representative of the period. Convenience of the reader was another consideration; the dramas from which examples are drawn are in general easily accessible in books which any reasonably well equipped reference library may be expected to possess.

On the whole the passages listed are rather long because, while shorter passages illustrating the same methods are much more numerous, the longer ones usually have the advantage of carrying the convention forward to a more extreme degree of mechanization and of displaying it more clearly and completely. The dates given below are taken from E. K. Chambers' *The Elizabethan Stage*, except those of Shakespeare's plays, which are from the same author's *William Shakespeare*. The captions here follow the order observed in Chapter II. Certain well-known editions of plays are referred to in the table by abbreviations, as follows:

CED — *The Chief Elizabethan Dramatists*, edited by W. A. Neilson
CPD — *Chief Pre-Shakespearean Dramas*, edited by J. Q. Adams
CW — *The Complete Works of John Lyly*, edited by R. W. Bond
REC — *Representative English Comedies*, edited by C. M. Gayley
SCE — *Shakespeare's Complete Works*, Student's Cambridge Edition, edited by W. A. Neilson
SPD — *Specimens of the Pre-Shakespearean Drama*, edited by J. M. Manly

I. DIRECT SELF-IDENTIFICATION

1. Lyly, *Sapho and Phao* (1584), I, 1, 1–4, 19–24. Bond, CW.
2. Shakespeare, *The Taming of the Shrew* (1593–94), II, i, 41–70. Neilson, SCE.
3. Dekker, *The Shomakers Holiday* (1599), I, i, 127–128. Gayley, REC.
4. Jonson, *Every Man out of His Humour* (1599), I, i, Mermaid Series, I, 129.
5. Shakespeare, *Twelfth Night* (1599–1600), II, i, 12–25. Neilson, SCE.
6. Shakespeare, *Troilus and Cressida* (1601–2), I, iii, 31–33, 54–55, 58, 68–69. Neilson, SCE.
7. Jonson, *Volpone* (1606), II, i, 25. Neilson, CED.
8. Shakespeare, *Cymbeline* (1609–10), III, iii, 106. Neilson, SCE.

9. Shakespeare, *The Winter's Tale* (1610–11), IV, iii, 23–32. Neilson, SCE.

II. AUTOBIOGRAPHIC SELF-IDENTIFICATION

1. Greene, *James the Fourth* (*c.* 1591), "Induction," lines 34–69. Manly, SPD.
2. Peele, *The Old Wives Tale* (1591 to 1594), lines 212–227. Neilson, CED.
3. Shakespeare, *The Comedy of Errors* (1592–93), I, i, 37–58. Neilson, SCE.
4. Shakespeare, *The Taming of the Shrew* (1593–94), "Induction," ii, 5–26. Neilson, SCE.
5. Haughton? *Grim, the Collier of Croydon* (1600), Scene i. Hazlitt, *Dodsley's Old English Plays*, Fourth Edition (1874), VIII, 391–393.
6. Shakespeare, *The Tempest* (1611–12), I, ii, 22–184. Neilson, SCE.

III. DIRECT SELF-CHARACTERIZATION

1. Greene? *George a Greene, the Pinner of Wakefield* (not later than 1593), lines 99–112. Adams, CPD.
2. Shakespeare, *The Taming of the Shrew* (1593–94), I, ii, 48–76, 93–96, 191–211. Neilson, SCE.
3. Shakespeare, *The Merchant of Venice* (1596–97), I, i, 1–7, 15–45, 76–86; II, i, 1–7, 24–30. Neilson, SCE.
4. Dekker, *Old Fortunatus* (1599), I, i. Mermaid Series, pp. 293–294.
5. Dekker, *The Honest Whore*, Part II (*c.* 1605), I, ii, 51–99. Neilson, CED.
6. Jonson, *Volpone* (1606), I, i, 1–13, 30–40. Neilson, CED.
7. Middleton, *A Chaste Maid in Cheapside* (1611), I, ii. Mermaid Series, I, 182–183.

IV. DIRECT SELF-CHARACTERIZATION SUPPLEMENTED
BY A CHORUS

1. Shakespeare, *As You Like It* (1599–1600), III, ii, 21–81. Neilson, SCE.
2. Anonymous, *The Merry Devill of Edmonton* (*c.* 1603), I, iii, 95–111. Gayley, REC.
3. Thos. Heywood, *The Wise-Woman of Hogsdon* (*c.* 1604?), II, i. Mermaid Series, pp. 265–268.
4. Day, *Humour out of Breath* (1607–8), I, i. Mermaid Series, *Nero and Other Plays*, pp. 275–276.
5. Shakespeare, *Cymbeline* (1609–10), I, ii, 1–39. Neilson, SCE.

6. Beaumont and Fletcher, *Philaster* (not later than 1610), I, i. Mermaid Series, I, 107–108.
7. Beaumont and Fletcher, *A King and No King* (1611), I, i. Mermaid Series, II, 9–10.

V. PRELIMINARY DIRECT CHARACTERIZATION

1. Lyly, *Campaspe* (1584), I, ii, 1–26. Bond, CW.
2. Shakespeare, *Love's Labour's Lost* (1594–95), I, i, 163–179. Neilson, SCE.
3. Shakespeare, *Twelfth Night* (1599–1600), I, i, 19–39; I, ii, 35–41. Neilson, SCE.
4. Dekker, *The Honest Whore*, Part I (1604), I, ii, 75–133; I, iv, 9–33. Neilson, CED.
5. Middleton, *A Trick to Catch the Old One* (1604 to 1606), I, i. Mermaid Series, I, 5–9.
6. Jonson, *The Alchemist* (1610), I, iv, 6–29. Gayley, REC.

VI. DIRECT CHARACTERIZATION IMMEDIATELY PRECEDING FIRST APPEARANCE

1. Dekker, *The Shomakers Holiday* (1599), I, i, 17–35, 46–50. Gayley, REC.
2. Shakespeare, *As You Like It* (1599–1600), I, i, 1–30. Neilson, SCE.
3. Dekker and Webster, *Westward Ho!* (1604), II, i. Alexander Dyce, ed., *John Webster*, p. 215.
4. Day, *Humour out of Breath* (1607–8), I, ii. Mermaid Series, *Nero and Other Plays*, p. 279.
5. Fletcher, *The Faithful Shepherdess* (1608–9), I, ii. Mermaid Series, *Beaumont and Fletcher*, II, 333.
6. Jonson, *Epicœne* (1609), I, iii, 22–49. Gayley, REC.
7. Shakespeare, *The Tempest* (1611–12), I, ii, 307–320. Neilson, SCE.

VII. DIRECT CHARACTERIZATION DURING OR SUBSEQUENT TO FIRST APPEARANCE

1. Lyly, *Mother Bombie* (1587 to 1590), II, iii, 16–75. Bond, CW.
2. Jonson, *Every Man in His Humour* (1598), I, iv, 74–92. Neilson, CED.
3. Shakespeare, *All's Well That Ends Well* (1602–3), I, i, 109–116. Neilson, SCE.

4. Shakespeare, *Troilus and Cressida* (1601–2), I, ii, 202–260. Neilson, SCE.
5. Dekker and Webster, *Northward Ho!* (1605), I, i, Dyce's *Webster*, p. 249.
6. Shakespeare, *Cymbeline* (1609–10), III, iii, 79–98. Neilson, SCE.
7. Thos. Heywood, *The Fair Maid of the West* (ideas as to date vary from late Elizabethan times to approximately 1617; Chambers does not list the play), I, iii. Mermaid Series, p. 85.
8. Beaumont and Fletcher, *Philaster* (not later than 1610), I, i. Mermaid Series, I, 104–105.

VIII.   LATER DIRECT CHARACTERIZATION

1. Porter, *The Two Angry Women of Abington* (not later than 1598), v, 10–25, 31–39. Gayley, REC.
2. Shakespeare, *Much Ado about Nothing* (1598–99), II, i, 254–255, 258–268. Neilson, SCE.
3. Dekker, *The Shomakers Holiday* (1599), I, i, 163–169. Gayley, REC.
4. Shakespeare, *The Merry Wives of Windsor* (1600–1), IV, ii, 21–28. Neilson, SCE.
5. Anonymous, *The Merry Devill of Edmonton* (c. 1603), I, iii, 106–111. Gayley, REC.
6. Shakespeare, *Measure for Measure* (1604–5), I, iv, 57–61. Neilson, SCE.
7. Middleton, *A Chaste Maid in Cheapside* (1611), V, iv. Mermaid Series, I, 252–253.

IX.   NARRATIVE FOR PURPOSES OF CHARACTERIZATION

1. Lyly, *Campaspe* (1584), I, iii, 1–24. Bond, CW.
2. Greene? *George a Greene, the Pinner of Wakefield* (not later than 1593), lines 393–435. Adams, CPD.
3. Shakespeare, *The Taming of the Shrew* (1593–94), II, i, 145–160; III, ii, 151–184. Neilson, SCE.
4. Jonson, *Every Man out of His Humour* (1599), IV, ii. Mermaid Series, I, 215–217.
5. Shakespeare, *As You Like It* (1599–1600), II, i, 25–66. Neilson, SCE.
6. Day, *Humour out of Breath* (1607–8), I, i. Mermaid Series, *Nero and Other Plays*, p. 276.
7. Field, *A Woman is a Weathercock* (1609?), I, i. Mermaid Series, *Nero and Other Plays*, p. 345.

X. CHARACTER VERIFIES GENUINE CHANGE OF HIS
OWN ATTITUDE

1. Greene, *Frier Bacon and Frier Bungay* (*c.* 1589), viii, 112–121. Gayley, REC.
2. Lyly, *Midas* (1589–90), III, i, 1–64. Bond, CW.
3. Shakespeare, *The Two Gentlemen of Verona* (1594–95), II, iv, 192–214. Neilson, SCE.
4. Shakespeare, *A Midsummer-Night's Dream* (1595–96), II, i, 146–185, with IV, i, 49–66. Neilson, SCE.
5. Dekker, *The Honest Whore*, Part II (*c.* 1605), I, ii, 208–225. Neilson, CED.
6. Shakespeare, *The Winter's Tale* (1610–11), I, ii, 1–350. Neilson, SCE.

XI. CHARACTER INTERPRETS FEIGNED CHANGE OF
HIS OWN ATTITUDE

1. Lyly, *Endimion* (1588), IV, i, 72–79. Bond, CW.
2. Shakespeare, *The Merchant of Venice* (1596–97), I, iii, 40–61. Neilson, SCE.
3. Porter, *The Two Angry Women of Abington* (not later than 1598), vi, 132–207. Gayley, REC.
4. Shakespeare, *Troilus and Cressida* (1601–2), I, ii, 308–321. Neilson, SCE.
5. Middleton, *A Trick to Catch the Old One* (1604 to 1606), II, i. Mermaid Series, I, 22–23, 25.
6. Middleton and Dekker, *The Roaring Girl* (*c.* 1610), I, i; II, ii. Mermaid Series, *Thomas Middleton*, II, 10–11, 41–42.

XII. INTERPRETATION SUPPLIED BY CHORUS AT TIME OF
CHANGE OF ATTITUDE

1. Shakespeare, *The Two Gentlemen of Verona* (1594–95), II, i, 100–181. Neilson, SCE.
2. Shakespeare, *Troilus and Cressida* (1601–2), IV, v, 54–63. Neilson, SCE.
3. Thos. Heywood, *The Royal King and Loyal Subject* (1602?), I, i; II, i; IV, i. *Old English Plays*, being a Continuation of Dodsley (London, 1816), VI, 239, 252, 300–302.
4. Shakespeare, *Measure for Measure* (1604–5), II, ii, 25–161. Neilson, SCE.

5. Dekker and Webster, *Northward Ho!* (1605), V, i. Dyce's *Webster*, pp. 278–279.
6. Middleton, *Michaelmas Term* (1606?), II, iii, 103–389. Masterpieces of the English Drama.
7. Shakespeare, *The Tempest* (1611–12), III, iii, 104–109. Neilson, SCE.
8. Beaumont and Fletcher, *A King and No King* (1611), III, iii; IV, ii. Mermaid Series II, 56, 68–69.

*
*   *

Epithetic Direct Characterization

A device which may be called "epithetic direct characterization" is so offhand and desultory that it seems not to merit detailed consideration, and yet it is of sufficient importance to receive brief mention here. It is the simple, universal, and fragmentary, but highly satisfactory, process of describing a character by calling him names, by applying to him appropriate terse nouns or adjectives.

Chapman makes extensive use of epithetic characterization. In *All Fools* Valerio speaks of his father's "covetous humour,"[1] and Rinaldo refers to the same old gentleman as "your frowning father,"[2] thereby indicating that Gostanzo is a typical stern parent. Rinaldo later calls Gostanzo "this old, politic, dissembling knight."[3] Speaking of Valerio, Cornelio asks: ". . . shall we gull this guller?"[4] In *The Gentleman Usher* another stock figure is branded in a command of Duke Alphonso's: "Good Master Pedant, pray forth with your show."[5] In *May-Day* Angelo calls Lorenzo a "notable old whinyard,"[6] and Fannio, with Quintiliano's assault upon Innocentio's purse in mind, remarks: "I hope he will foist some money for my score out of this gull here."[7] In *An Humour-*

---

[1] *All Fools*, I, i, 137.
[2] *Ibid.*, I, ii, 104.
[3] *Ibid.*, I, i, 401.
[4] *Ibid.*, II, i, 367.
[5] *The Gentleman Usher*, II, i, 271.
[6] *May-Day*, I, i, 51.
[7] *Ibid.*, I, i, 320–321.

ous Day's Mirth Colinet speaks of Blanuel as "this gallant."[8] In nine consecutive lines of *The Widow's Tears* two of Eudora's maids classify two characters, Arsace as a pandress, and Argus as "that bold ass, that never weighs what he does or says, but walks and talks like one in a sleep."[9] Countless illustrations might easily be added to these few.

The widespread use of this convenient, keen, forceful, and frequently mocking characterization among other dramatists of the period may be suggested by the following references:

1. Lyly, *Campaspe* (1584), I, ii, 1–2, 7. Bond, CW.
2. Greene, *James the Fourth* (*c.* 1591), V, vi, 142. Manly, SPD.
3. Peele, *David and Bethsabe* (not later than 1594), I, i, 79. Manly, SPD.
4. Jonson, *Every Man in His Humour* (1598), I, i, 62. Neilson, CED.
5. Shakespeare, *The Merry Wives of Windsor* (1600–1), II, i, 23–25, 64–66, 111–112. Neilson, SCE.
6. Shakespeare, *Twelfth Night* (1599–1600), II, v, 5–7. Neilson, SCE.

*

* *

IDENTIFICATION OF DISGUISED FIGURES

1. Greene, *James the Fourth* (*c.* 1591), III, iii, 99–112, 119–121, 128; IV, iv, 1–14. Manly, SPD.
2. Shakespeare, *The Two Gentlemen of Verona* (1594–95), II, vii, 39–43. Neilson, SCE.
3. Shakespeare, *The Merchant of Venice* (1596–97), III, iv, 58–64, 78. Neilson, SCE.
4. Dekker, *The Shomakers Holiday* (1599), II, ii, 1–6. Gayley, REC.
5. Shakespeare, *The Merry Wives of Windsor* (1600–1), IV, ii, 67–81, 174–179, 201–205. Neilson, SCE.
6. Shakespeare, *As You Like It* (1599–1600), I, iii, 113–135; II, iv, 1–10. Neilson, SCE.
7. Shakespeare, *Twelfth Night* (1599–1600), I, ii, 52–56, 62; II, i, 1–11. Neilson, SCE.

[8] *An Humourous Day's Mirth*, ii, 33.
[9] *The Widow's Tears*, II, ii, 1–9. Tharsalio has earlier (I, ii, 121–122) described Arsace in his cynical fashion as "the virtuous pandress Arsace."

8. Anonymous, *The Merry Devill of Edmonton* (*c.* 1603), II, ii, 76–100; II, iii, 68–78; III, ii, 1–25, 71–88. Gayley, REC.

9. Thos. Heywood, *The Wise-Woman of Hogsdon* (*c.* 1604?), I, ii, Mermaid Series, pp. 263–264.

10. Dekker, *The Honest Whore*, Part II (*c.* 1605), I, iii, 233–257. Neilson, CED.

11. Shakespeare, *Cymbeline* (1609–10), III, iv, 168–196; III, vi, 1–3. Neilson, SCE.

12. Jonson, *Bartholomew Fair* (1614), II, i; V, i; V, ii. Mermaid Series, II, 37, 125, 126.

APPENDIX D

COEFFETEAU AND OTHERS ON THE
HUMAN SYSTEM

THE following passages are important as summarizing the theories of physiology outlined in Chapter VII:

"As soone as the *Exterior sences*, busied about the *Objects* which are proper for them, have gathered the formes of things which come from without, they carry them to the *common sence*, the which receives them, judgeth of them, and distinguisheth them; and then to preserve them in the absence of their objects, presents them to the Imagination, which having gathered them together, to the end she may represent them whensoever need shall require, she delivers them to the custody of the *Memory*; from whence retiring them when occasion requires, she propounds them unto the *Appetite*, under the apparance of things that are pleasing or troublesom, that is to say, under the *forme* of *Good* and *Evill*; and at the same instant the *formes* enlightened with the *Light* of the *understanding*, and purged from the *sensible* and singular conditions, which they retained in the *Imagination*, and instead of that which they represented of particular things, representing them generall, they become capable to be imbraced by the *understanding*; the which under the apparance of things which are profitable or hurtfull, that is to say, under the *forme* of *Good* or *Evill*, represents them unto the *Will*: the which being blind referres it selfe to that which the *understanding* proposeth unto it: and then as *Queene* of the powers of the soule she ordaines what they shall imbrace, & what they shall fly as it pleseth her; Whereunto the *Sensitive Appetite* yeelding a prompt obedience to execute her command, from the which it never straies, so long as it containes it selfe within the bounds and order prescrib'd by *Nature*, quickneth all the powers and *passions* over which shee commands, and sets to worke those which are necessary to that action, and by this meanes commands the moving *power*, dispersed over all the members, to follow or fly, to approch or recoyle, or to do any other motion which it requireth. And shee obeying suddenly if shee bee not hindred, moves, the whole body with the Organs, which reside in the parts, and induceth them to fly or imbrace things according to the command which she hath received.

"After this manner *Man* proceeds in his free *operations*, if he will observe the order which he ought. The which I say, for that oftentimes hee overthrows and perverts this order, either by bad education, or by *custome*, or the *organs* being unsound, or for that his *will* hath bad inclination; so as *reason* cannot enjoy her *power*, & subject the *Sensuall Appetite* unto her; but contrariwise hee abandons himselfe in prey unto this disordered *Appetite*, and suffers himselfe to bee transported by his furious motions. So as suddenly when as fantasie offers to the *Appetite*, the *formes* which shee receives from the *Sences*, under the shew of *Good* or *Evill*; he without stay to have them judged by the discourse of *understanding*, and chosen by the *will*, commands of himself the moving *power*, & makes it to act according to his pleasure. And herein consistes the disorder which the *passions* cause in the life of man, which divert him many times from the lawes of *Reason*."[1]

"This Spirit [i.e. the animal spirits] is the chiefe instrument, and immediate, whereby the soule bestoweth the exercises of her facultie in her bodie, that passeth to and fro in a moment, nothing in swiftnesse and nimblenesse being comparable thereunto: which when it is depraved by any occa-

[1] F. N. Coeffeteau, *A Table of Humane Passions*, Preface (no pagination).

sion, either rising from the bodie, or by other meanes, then becometh it an instrument unhandsome for the performance of such actions, as require the use thereof: and so the minde seemeth to be blame worthie, wherein it is blamelesse: and faultie of certaine actions imputed thereunto: wherein the bodie and this Spirit are rather to bee charged, things corporall and Earthly."[2]

"*Sleep is a rest or binding of the outward senses, and of the common sense, for the preservation of body and soul* . . . for when the common sense resteth, the outward senses rest also. The phantasy alone is free, and his commander, reason: as appears by those imaginary dreams, which are of divers kinds, *natural, divine, demoniacal, &c.* . . . This ligation of senses proceeds from an inhibition of spirits, the way being stopped by which they should come; this stopping is caused of vapours arising out of the stomack, filling the nerves, by which the [animal] spirits would be conveyed. When these vapours are spent, the passage is open, and the spirits perform their accustomed duties; so that *waking is the action and motion of the senses, which the spirits dispersed over all parts cause.*"[3]

"Sleepe is a surceasing of all the sences from trauel, which is, or is caused by certayne euaporations and fumes rysing of our meate and sustenance receyued, mounting from the stomacke immediately into the brayne, by whose great coldnesse these vapours warme are tempered, casting into a slumber euerye the forces, or sences exterior; at which time the vitall spirites, retiring to the heart, leaue all the members of the bodye in a sleepe, vntill suche time againe as these sayde vitall spirites recouer new force and strength to them againe; and so these vapors, or ceasing, or diminishing, man againe

[2] Timothy Bright, *A Treatise of Melancholy*, p. 43.
[3] Robert Burton, *The Anatomy of Melancholy*, I, 182–183.

awaketh, and returneth to himselfe more apt to his businesse
than at any time before."[4]

[4] John Northbrooke, *A Treatise wherein Dicing, Dauncing, Vaine
Playes, or Enterluds, with other idle Pastimes &c., commonly vsed on the
Sabboth Day, are reproued by the Authoritie of the Word of God and
auntiant Writers.* Originally entered for publication in 1577, it was
edited for the Shakespeare Society by J. P. Collier in 1843. The quota-
tion is from page 38 of the Collier edition. With this passage and the
preceding one compare Chapman's *The Revenge of Bussy D'Ambois*
(1610–11), V, i, 41–53.

BIBLIOGRAPHY

BIBLIOGRAPHY

ACHESON, ARTHUR, *Shakespeare and the Rival Poet*. John Lane, London and New York, 1903.

ADAMS, JOSEPH QUINCY, ed., *Chief Pre-Shakespearean Dramas*. Houghton Mifflin Company, Cambridge (Mass.), 1924.

ANDERSON, RUTH L., *Elizabethan Psychology and Shakespeare's Plays*, University of Iowa Studies, Humanistic Series, Vol. III, No. 4. University of Iowa, Iowa City, 1927.

ARCHER, WILLIAM, *The Old Drama and the New*. Small, Maynard and Company, Boston, 1923.

——*Play-Making*. Small, Maynard and Company, Boston, 1912.

ARNOLD, MORRIS LEROY, *The Soliloquies of Shakespeare*. Columbia University Press, New York, 1911.

AYRES, HARRY MORGAN, "Chapman's *Homer* and Others," *The* [*New York*] *Nation*, 104, No. 2702 (April 12, 1917), 439–441.

BASKERVILL, CHARLES R., *English Elements in Jonson's Early Comedy*, University of Texas Bulletin No. 178. University of Texas, Austin, Texas, 1911.

BEATTY, ARTHUR B., "The St. George, or Mummers', Plays: a Study in the Protology of the Drama," *Bulletin of the Wisconsin Academy of Sciences, Arts, and Letters*, 15, Part 2 (1907), 273–324.

BOAS, FREDERICK S., "The Source of Chapman's *The Conspiracie and Tragedie of Charles, Duke of Byron*, and *The Revenge of Bussy D'Ambois*," *Athenaeum*, Issue No. 3924 (Jan. 10, 1903), 51–52.

——*University Drama in the Tudor Age*. Clarendon Press, Oxford, 1914.

BOND, R. WARWICK, ed., *Early Plays from the Italian*. Clarendon Press, Oxford, 1911.

BRIGHT, TIMOTHY ("Doctor of Phisicke"), *A Treatise of Melancholy*, Newly Corrected and Amended (containing the Epistle Dedicatory to the edition of 1586). William Stansby, London, 1613.

BROOKE, C. F. TUCKER, *The Tudor Drama*. Houghton Mifflin Company, Boston and New York, 1911.

BROWNE, WILLIAM, *The Poems of William Browne*, edited by Gordon Goodwin, with an introduction by A. H. Bullen, two volumes. Lawrence and Bully, London; Charles Scribner's Sons, New York, 1894.

BRUNETIÈRE, FERDINAND, "La Loi du théâtre," printed as a preface to Édouard Noël and Edmond Stoullig's *Les Annales du théâtre et de la musique*. Bibliothéque-Charpentier, Paris, 1894.

BULLEN, ARTHUR HENRY, *Elizabethans*. Chapman and Hall, London, 1924.

——"George Chapman," *The Dictionary of National Biography*, edited by Leslie Stephen and Sidney Lee, X, 47–53. Smith, Elder, and Company, London, 1887.

BUNDY, MURRAY W., "Shakespeare and Elizabethan Psychology," *JEGP*, XXIII (1924), 516–549.

BURTON, ROBERT, *The Anatomy of Melancholy*, edited by the Rev. A. R. Shilleto, three volumes. George Bell and Sons, London and New York, 1893.

BUSBY, OLIVE M., *Studies in the Development of the Fool in Elizabethan Drama*. Humphrey Milford, Oxford University Press, London and New York, 1923.

BUTLER, SAMUEL, *Characters and Passages from Note-Books*, edited by A. R. Waller. University Press, Cambridge, 1908.

CAMPBELL, OSCAR JAMES, JR., *The Comedies of Holberg*. Harvard University Press, Cambridge (Mass.), 1914.

——"The Italianate Background of *The Merry Wives of Windsor*," *Essays and Studies in English and Comparative Literature*, by members of the English Department of the University of Michigan, University of Michigan Publications, Language and Literature, VIII, 81–117. University of Michigan Press, Ann Arbor, 1932.

——"*Love's Labour's Lost* Re-studied," *Studies in Shakespeare, Milton, and Donne*, by members of the English Department of the University of Michigan, University of Michigan Publications, Language and Literature, I, 3–45. Macmillan, New York and London, 1925. (This volume may be purchased from the University of Michigan only.)

——"*The Two Gentlemen of Verona* and Italian Comedy," *Studies in Shakespeare, Milton, and Donne*, I, 49–63. (For bibliographical data see the last entry.)

CASTELAIN, MAURICE, *Ben Jonson*; *l'homme et l'œuvre*. Librairie Hachette et Cie, Paris and London, 1907.

CHAMBERS, EDMUND K., *The Elizabethan Stage*, four volumes. Clarendon Press, Oxford, 1923.

——"Italian Players in England," *LTLS*, Issue No. 1008 (May 12, 1921), 307.

——*The Mediaeval Stage*, two volumes. Clarendon Press, Oxford, 1903.

——*William Shakespeare*, two volumes. Clarendon Press, Oxford, 1930.

CHAPMAN, GEORGE, *"All Fooles"* and *"The Gentleman Usher,"* edited by Thomas Marc Parrott for the Belles-Lettres Series. D. C. Heath and Company, Boston and London, 1907.

——*Alphonsus, Emperor of Germany*, edited by Herbert F. Schwartz. G. P. Putnam's Sons, New York and London, 1913.

——*"Bussy D'Ambois"* and *"The Revenge of Bussy D'Ambois,"* edited by Frederick S. Boas for the Belles-Lettres Series. D. C. Heath and Company, Boston and London, 1905.

——*Charlemagne* (*The Distracted Emperor*), edited by Franck L. Schoell. Princeton University Press, Princeton; Humphrey Milford, London, 1920.

——*The Comedies and Tragedies of George Chapman* [edited by R. H. Shepherd]. J. Pearson, London, 1873.

——*George Chapman*, edited by William Lyon Phelps for the Mermaid Series. T. Fisher Unwin, London; Charles Scribner's Sons, New York, 1895.

——*The Plays and Poems of George Chapman: The Comedies*, edited by Thomas Marc Parrott. George Routledge and Sons, London; E. P. Dutton and Company, New York, 1914.

——*The Plays and Poems of George Chapman: The Tragedies*, edited by Thomas Marc Parrott. George Routledge and Sons, London; E. P. Dutton and Company, New York, 1910.

——*Sir Gyles Goosecappe nach der Quarto 1606 in Neudruck hrsg. von W. Band und R. Brotanek*. A. Uystpruyst, Louvain, 1919.

——*Two Wise Men and All the Rest Fools*, issued by the editor of the Tudor Facsimile Texts, 1913.

——*The Tragedie of Chabot, Admirall of France*, reprinted from the Quarto of 1639, edited by Ezra Lehman, Publications of the University of Pennsylvania, Series in Philology and Literature, Vol. X. John C. Winston Company, Philadelphia, 1916.

——*The Works of George Chapman*: *Plays*, edited by Richard Herne Shepherd. Chatto and Windus, London, 1874.

——*The Works of George Chapman*: *Poems and Minor Translations*, edited by Algernon Charles Swinburne. Chatto and Windus, London, 1875.

CHARRON, PIERRE, *Of Wisdom*, translated from Charron's *De la sagesse* by Samson Lennard. Printed for Nathaniel Ranew and Jonathan Robinson, London, 1670.

COEFFETEAU, F. N., *A Table of Humane Passions*, translated by Edward Grimeston. Nicholas Okes, London, 1621.

COLLIER, JOHN PAYNE, *The History of English Dramatic Poetry and Annals of the Stage*, three volumes. George Bell and Sons, London, 1879.

COURTHOPE, WILLIAM J., *A History of English Poetry*, six volumes. Macmillan and Company, London, 1911.

CREIZENACH, WILHELM, *The English Drama in the Age of Shakespeare*, translated from Vol. IV, Books 1–8, of Creizenach's *Geschichte des neueren Dramas*, by Miss Cécile Hugon. Sidgwick and Jackson, London, 1916.

CUNLIFFE, JOHN W., "The Influence of Italian on Early Elizabethan Drama," *MP*, IV (1907), 597–604.

CUSHMAN, LYSANDER W., "The Devil and the Vice in the English Dramatic Literature before Shakespeare," *Studien zur englischen Philologie*, Vol. VI, 1900.

DAVIES, JOHN, OF HEREFORD, *The Complete Works of John Davies of Hereford*, edited by the Rev. Alexander B. Grosart for the Chértsie Worthies Library, two volumes. University Press, Edinburgh, 1878.

DAVIS, WILLIAM STEARNS, *Life in Elizabethan Days*. Harper and Brothers, New York and London, 1930.

DEKKER, THOMAS, *The Best Plays of Thomas Dekker*, edited by Ernest Rhys for the Mermaid Series. T. Fisher Unwin, London; Charles Scribner's Sons, New York [1894].

——*The Guls Hornbook and the Belman of London*, in The Temple Classics. J. M. Dent and Company, London, 1904.

DE ROTHSCHILD, JAMES A., *Shakespeare and His Day*. Edward Arnold, London, 1906.

DIXON, W. MACNEILE, "Chapman, Marston, Dekker," *The Cambridge History of English Literature* (Cambridge, University Press, 1910), VI, 33–65.

DOBELL, BERTRAM, "Newly Discovered Documents of the Elizabethan and Jacobean Periods. Letters and Documents by George Chapman," *Athenaeum*, Issue No. 3830 (March 23, 1901), 369–370; Issue No. 3831 (March 30, 1901), 403–404; Issue No. 3832 (April 6, 1901), 433–434; Issue No. 3833 (April 13, 1901), 465–467.

DODSLEY, ROBERT, *A Select Collection of Old English Plays*, Fourth Edition, edited by William C. Hazlitt, fifteen volumes. Reeves and Turner, London, 1874–76.

DOWDEN, EDWARD, "Elizabethan Psychology," *Essays: Modern and Elizabethan*, pp. 308–333. J. M. Dent and Company, London; E. P. Dutton and Company, New York, 1910.

DRYDEN, JOHN, *The Works of John Dryden*, edited by Sir Walter Scott and by George Saintsbury, eighteen volumes. W. Paterson, Edinburgh, 1882–93.

DUCHARTRE, PIERRE LOUIS, *La Comédie italienne*. Librarie de France, Paris, 1924, translated by R. T. Weaver and published as *The Italian Comedy*. George G. Harrap and Company, Ltd., London, 1929.

EARLE, JOHN, *Microcosmographie; or, A Piece of the World Discovered in Essays and Characters*, in The Temple Classics. J. M. Dent and Company, London, 1899.

ECKHARDT, EDUARD, "Die lustige Person im älteren englischen Drama," *Palaestra*, Vol. XVII, 1902.

EINSTEIN, LEWIS, *The Italian Renaissance in England*. Columbia University Press, New York, 1903.

FERGUSON, A. S., "The Plays of George Chapman," *MLR*, XIII (1918), 1–24.

FEUILLERAT, ALBERT, ed., *Documents Relating to the Office of the Revels in the Time of Queen Elizabeth*, Materialen zur Kunde des älteren englischen Dramas, hrsg. von W. Bang, 21 bd. A. Uystpruyst, Louvain, 1908.

FLEAY, FREDERICK GARD, *A Biographical Chronicle of the English Drama, 1559–1642*, two volumes. Reeves and Turner, London, 1891.

FORSYTHE, ROBERT S., *The Relations of Shirley's Plays to the Elizabethan Drama.* Columbia University Press, New York, 1914.

FREEBURG, V. O., *Disguise Plots in Elizabethan Drama.* Columbia University Press, 1915.

GAYLEY, CHARLES MILLS, *Plays of Our Forefathers.* Duffield and Company, New York, 1907.

——ed., *Representative English Comedies,* three volumes. Macmillan, New York and London, 1903, 1913, 1914.

GREENE, ROBERT, AND PEELE, GEORGE, *The Dramatic and Poetical Works of Robert Greene and George Peele,* edited by the Rev. Alexander Dyce for the Old Dramatists and the Old Poets Series. George Routledge and Sons, London, and New York, n. d.

HAMILTON, CLAYTON, *Problems of the Playwright.* Henry Holt and Company, New York, 1917.

HENRY, G. KENNETH G., "The Characters of Terence," *SP,* XII (1915), 57–98.

HENSLOWE, PHILIP, *Henslowe's Diary,* edited by Walter W. Greg, Part I, *The Text;* Part II, *The Commentary.* A. H. Bullen, London, 1904, 1908.

——*Henslowe's Papers,* edited by Walter W. Greg. A. H. Bullen, London, 1907.

JONSON, BEN, *Ben Jonson,* edited by Charles H. Herford and Brinsley Nicholson for the Mermaid Series, three volumes. T. Fisher Unwin, London; Charles Scribner's Sons, New York [1903].

——*Ben Jonson,* edited by Charles H. Herford and Percy Simpson, in progress. Clarendon Press, Oxford, 1925—.

——*Every Man in His Humour,* edited by Percy Simpson. Clarendon Press, Oxford, 1919.

JUDGES, A. V., ed., *The Elizabethan Underworld.* E. P. Dutton and Company, New York, 1930.

KERR, MINA, *The Influence of Ben Jonson on English Comedy, 1598–1642.* D. Appleton and Company, New York, 1912.

KOEPPEL, EMIL, "Quellen-Studien zu den Dramen George Chapman's, Philip Massinger's, und John Ford's," *Quellen und Forschungen zur Sprach- und Culturgeschichte der germanischen Völker.* Karl J. Trübner, Strassburg, 1897.

KREIDER, PAUL V., "Gloucester's Eyes," *Shakespeare Association Bulletin*, VIII (1933), 121–132.

——"The Mechanics of Disguise in Shakespeare's Plays," *ibid.*, IX (1934), 167–180.

LAWRENCE, WILLIAM W., "The Meaning of *All's Well That Ends Well*," *PMLA*, XXXVII (1922), 418–469.

LEA, K. M., *Italian Popular Comedy*, two volumes. Clarendon Press, Oxford, 1934.

LEE, SIDNEY LAZARUS, "Chapman's *Amorous Zodiacke*," *MP*, III (1905), 143–158.

——*The French Renaissance in England*. Clarendon Press, Oxford, 1910.

LOWELL, JAMES RUSSELL, "George Chapman," *Early Prose Writings of James Russell Lowell*, with a prefatory note by Dr. Hale and an introductory note by Walter Littlefield. John Lane, London and New York, 1903.

LYLY, JOHN, *The Complete Works of John Lyly*, edited by R. Warwick Bond, three volumes. Clarendon Press, Oxford, 1902.

MANLEY, JOHN MATTHEWS, ed., *Specimens of the Pre-Shakespearean Drama*, two volumes. Ginn and Company, Boston and London, 1897.

MATTHEWS, BRANDER, *A Study of the Drama*. Houghton Mifflin Company, Boston, New York, and Chicago, 1910.

——AND THORNDIKE, ASHLEY H., eds., *Shakesperian Studies*, by members of the Department of English and Comparative Literature in Columbia University. Columbia University Press, New York, 1916.

MOORE, JOHN BROOKS, *The Comic and the Realistic in English Drama*. University of Chicago Press, Chicago, 1925.

MUSTARD, W. P., "Hippocrates' Twins," *MLN*, XLI (1926), 50.

NASON, ARTHUR H., *James Shirley, Dramatist*. Published by the author, New York, 1915.

NEILSON, WILLIAM ALLAN, ed., *The Chief Elizabethan Dramatists*. Houghton Mifflin Company, Boston and New York, 1911.

——AND THORNDIKE, ASHLEY H., *The Facts about Shakespeare*, Revised Edition. The Macmillan Company, New York, 1931.

NORWOOD, GILBERT, *The Art of Terence*. Basil Blackwell, Oxford, 1923.

O'SULLIVAN, MARY I., "Hamlet and Dr. Timothy Bright," *PMLA*, XLI (1926), 667–679.

OVERBURY, SIR THOMAS, *The Miscellaneous Works in Prose and Verse of Sir Thomas Overbury, Knt.*, edited by Edward F. Rimbault. John Russell Smith, London, 1856.

PARROTT, THOMAS MARC, "The Authorship of *Sir Giles Goosecappe*," *MP*, IV (1906), 25–37.

——"The Authorship of *Two Italian Gentlemen*," *MP*, XIII (1915), 241–251.

——"Chapman and the Classics," *The* [*New York*] *Nation*, 88, No. 2285 (April 15, 1909), 381–382.

——"Notes on the Text of *Bussy D'Ambois*," *ESt*, XXXVIII (1907), 359–395.

——"Notes on the Text of Chapman's Plays. A. *Alphonsus, Emperor of Germany*," *Anglia*, XXX (1907), 349–379; "B. *Caeser and Pompey*," *ibid.*, pp. 501–522.

——"Notes on the Text of *The Revenge of Bussy D'Ambois* by George Chapman," *ESt*, XXXIX (1908), 70–82.

REINHARDSTÖTTNER, KARL VON, *Plautus: Spätere Bearbeitungen plautinischer Lustspiele*. Wilhelm Friedrich, Leipzig, 1886.

RISTINE, FRANK H., *English Tragicomedy*. Columbia University Press, New York, 1910.

ROBERTSON, JOHN M., *The Problems of the Shakespeare Sonnets*. George Routledge and Sons, London, 1926.

——*Shakespeare and Chapman*. T. Fisher Unwin, London, 1917.

ROBIN, PERCY ANSELL, *The Old Physiology in English Literature*. J. M. Dent and Sons, London; E. P. Dutton and Company, New York, 1911.

SAINTSBURY, GEORGE, *The Earlier Renaissance*. William Blackwood and Sons, Edinburgh and London, 1901.

SAND, MAURICE, *The History of the Harlequinade*, a translation of Sand's *Masques et Bouffons*, two volumes. Martin Secker, London; J. B. Lippincott Company, Philadelphia, 1915.

SCHELLING, FELIX E., *Elizabethan Drama, 1558–1642*, two volumes. Houghton Mifflin Company, Boston and New York, 1908.

——*English Literature during the Lifetime of Shakespeare*, Revised Edition. Henry Holt and Company, New York [1928].

——*Foreign Influences in Elizabethan Plays*. Harper and Brothers, New York and London, 1923.

SCHOELL, FRANCK L., "Les Emprunts de George Chapman à Marsile Ficin," *RLC*, jan-mar, 1922.

——*Études sur l'humanisme continental en Angleterre à la fin de la Renaissance*. Librairie Ancienne Honoré Champion, Paris, 1926.

——"George Chapman and the Italian Neo-Latinists of the Quattrocento," *MP*, XIII (1915), 215–238.

——"George Chapman's 'Commonplace Book,'" *MP*, XVII (1919), 199–218.

——"A New Source of *Sir Gyles Goosecappe*," *MP*, XI (1914), 547–558.

——AND ACHESON, ARTHUR, "Shakespeare, Chapman, et *Sir Thomas More*," *Revue anglo-américaine*, III (1926), 428–439, 514–531.

SCHÜCKING, LEVIN L., *Character Problems in Shakespeare's Plays*, translated from Schücking's *Die Charakterprobleme bei Shakespeare* by W. H. Peters. Henry Holt and Company, New York, 1922.

SHAKESPEARE, WILLIAM, *The Complete Works of William Shakespeare*, edited by William Allan Neilson, the Student's Cambridge Edition. Houghton Mifflin Company, Boston, 1906.

Shakespeare's England, by various authors, two volumes. Clarendon Press, Oxford, 1916.

SISSON, CHARLES J., *Le Goût public et le Théâtre élisabéthain jusqu'à la mort de Shakespeare*. Imprimerie Darantiere, Dijon [1922].

SMITH, G. GREGORY, ed., *Elizabethan Critical Essays*, two volumes. Clarendon Press, Oxford, 1904.

SMITH, WINIFRED, *The Commedia dell' arte*. Columbia University Press, New York, 1912.

SOLVE, NORMA DOBIE, *Stuart Politics in Chapman's "Tragedy of Chabot,"* University of Michigan Publications, Language and Literature, Vol. IV. University of Michigan Press, Ann Arbor, 1928.

SPENS, JANET, "Chapman's Ethical Thought," *Essays and Studies*, collected by Oliver Elton. Clarendon Press, Oxford, 1925.

SPINGARN, JOEL ELIAS, *A History of Literary Criticism in the Renaissance*. Columbia University Press, New York, 1912.

Stationers' Register, The, A Transcript of the Registers of the Company of Stationers of London, 1554–1660 A. D., edited by Edward Arber. Privately printed, London, 1875–1877, and Birmingham, 1894.

Stationers' Register, The, A Transcript of the Registers of the Worshipful Company of Stationers, 1640–1708 A. D., edited by G. E. Briscoe Eyre. Privately printed, London, 1913–1914.

STIEFEL, A. L., "George Chapman und das italienische Drama," *Shakespeare Jahrbuch*, XXXV (1899), 180–213.

STIER, MAX, *Chapman's "All Fools" mit besonderer Berücksichtigung seiner Quellen*. C. A. Kaemerer and Company, Halle, 1904.

STOLL, ELMER EDGAR, "Anachronism in Shakespeare Criticism," *MP*, VII (1910), 557–575.

——*Art and Artifice in Shakespeare*. University Press, Cambridge, 1933.

——"Falstaff," *MP*, XII (1914), 197–240.

——*Hamlet: An Historical and Comparative Study*, Studies in Language and Literature, No. 7, University of Minnesota, Minneapolis, 1919.

——"Hamlet and Iago," *Anniversary Papers*, by colleagues and pupils of George Lyman Kittredge, pp. 261–272. Ginn and Company, Boston and London, 1913.

——"The Objectivity of the Ghosts in Shakespeare," *PMLA*, XXII (1907), 201–233.

——"On the Date of Some of Chapman's Plays," *MLN*, XX (1905), 206–209.

——*Othello: An Historical and Comparative Study*, Studies in Language and Literature, No. 2, University of Minnesota, Minneapolis, 1915.

——*Shakespeare Studies*. The Macmillan Company, New York, 1927.

——"Shaksper, Marston, and the Malcontent Type," *MP*, III (1906), 281–303.

SWINBURNE, ALGERNON CHARLES, "Essay on the Poetical and Dramatic Works of George Chapman," *The Works of George Chapman: Poems and Minor Translations*, pp. ix-lxvii. Chatto and Windus, London, 1875.

TEMPE, ALLISON, "The Pater Noster Play and the Origin of the Vices," *PMLA*, XXXIX (1924), 789–804.

THOMAS, D. L., "The Authorship of *Revenge for Honour*," *MP*, V (1908), 617–636.

THORNDIKE, ASHLEY H., *English Comedy*. Macmillan, London and New York, 1929.

——*Shakespeare's Theatre*. The Macmillan Company, New York, 1916.

TILLEY, MORRIS P., "Recurrent Types of Confusion in Shakespeare's Clownish Dialogue," *Shakespeare Association Bulletin*, V (1930), 104–122.

——"A Variant of Homer's Story of Ulysses and the Sirens," *Classical Philology*, XXI (1926), 162–164.

VICARY, THOMAS, *The Anatomie of the Bodie of Man* (first published in 1548 and 1577), edited by Fredk. J. Furnivall and Percy Furnivall. The Early English Text Society, London, Extra Series No. LIII, 1888.

WARD, ADOLPHUS, *A History of English Dramatic Literature*, three volumes. Macmillan and Company, London, 1899.

WINSLOW, OLA ELIZABETH, *Low Comedy as a Structural Element in English Drama*. University of Chicago Press, Chicago, 1926.

WITHINGTON, ROBERT, "The Development of the 'Vice,' " *Essays in Memory of Barrett Wendell*, by his assistants, pp. 155–167. Harvard University Press, Cambridge (Mass.), 1926.

WOOD, ANTHONY À, *Athenae Oxonienses*, two volumes in one. T. Bennet, London, 1691–92.

WOODBRIDGE, ELIZABETH [Mrs. Morris], *The Drama: Its Law and Its Technique*. Allyn and Bacon, Boston and Chicago, 1898.

——*Studies in Jonson's Comedy*, Yale Studies in English, No. 5. Lamson, Wolffe and Company, Boston, New York, and London, 1898.

——"An Unnoted Source of Chapman's *All Fools*," *JGP*, I (1897), 338–341.

YOUNG, KARL, "The Influence of French Farce upon the Plays of John Heywood," *MP*, II (1904), 97–124.

INDEX

INDEX

(Cross references under "Characters, type" and "Psychology, Elizabethan" are to subentries under the same headings and not to other main entries.)

197